バイリンガルで読む

ラサール領事のなごや日記

The Canadian Consul LOVES Nagoya

著者：駐名古屋カナダ領事 シェニエ・ラサール

Foreword

Nagoya, December 8, 2019

I first came to Nagoya in 1994 on a Japanese Ministry of Education scholarship. I would end up living here for seven years, making many friends while studying and working in this great city. I would even get married to a Nagoya girl (a Seto girl to be precise) my wife Noriko, and our first two children, Sakura and Taro were born here. Our family left Nagoya for Tokyo in 2001 and a few years later in 2004, we all moved to Canada.

In 2016, I was named Canadian Consul in Nagoya and we all returned to the city where we first became a "family". My wife and kids were coming "home".

15 years had passed since we lived here. A lot had changed, but a lot of things — good things — were still the same. This book is about our family's rediscovery of this great city.

We love you Nagoya!

Chénier La Salle

はじめに
ラブレター・フロム・カナダ領事

はじめて名古屋に来たのは 1994 年、文部科学省の留学生受け入れ制度を利用してのことでした。

このすばらしい街で、学び、働き、多くの出会いを経て、気づけば 7 年もの月日が過ぎていました。名古屋の女性と（正確にいうと瀬戸出身の女性と）結婚もしました。妻の紀子との間にできた最初のふたりの子ども、さくらと太朗も、名古屋で生まれました。

2001 年に名古屋から東京に引っ越し、2004 年にはカナダへ移ったのですが、2016 年に在名古屋カナダ領事に任命され、私たち一家は、はじめて「家族」になったこの地にまた戻ってきました。

以前住んでいたころから 15 年が過ぎ、変わったこともたくさんありました。でも、変わっていないこともたくさんあり、特に名古屋のよいところはそのまま残っていました。この本はそんな私たち家族の、名古屋再発見の物語です。

愛する名古屋のみなさんへ、

シェニエ・ラサール

2019 年 12 月 8 日

本書は、中日新聞朝刊で 2017 年 11 月から 2018 年 4 月にかけて連載された「ラサールさんのなごや日記」およびその後身で名古屋に駐在する 6 カ国の領事が順番に執筆する「なごやか外交」の著者執筆記事に、加筆・修正したものです。

目次 contents

ラサール領事のなごや日記　La Salle's NAGOYA diary

NAGOYA, the center of Japan!

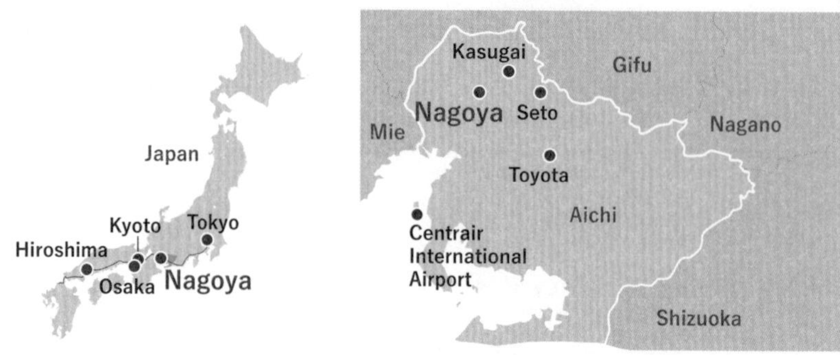

With a population of 2.33 million (2019), Nagoya, the capital of Aichi prefecture, is the largest city in the Chubu region and the 4th largest city in Japan. Nagoya is located in the center of Japan's main island of Honshu, and offers easy access to the rest of the country. When traveling by rail, Kyoto is only 35 minutes away via the "Shinkansen" bullet train and it will take you only 55 minutes to reach Osaka and 100 to reach Tokyo. You can also fly to Hokkaido or Okinawa from the Chubu Centrair International Airport. Direct train and bus service from Nagoya station make access to the airport very easy.

Aichi is the industrial heart of Japan and world-famous car manufacturer Toyota has its headquarters here. Nagoya is also a city rich in history. The powerful warlords who gradually unified the country waged decisive battles in the region and many icons of Japanese culture like the tea ceremony, Noh (classical musical drama) and traditional handicrafts (e.g. potteries, porcelains, tie-dyed fabrics) blossomed here.

There are 2.73 million foreigners living in Japan (2018), and about 10% of them live in Aichi. There are about 10,713 Canadians living in Japan of which about 650 live in Aichi.

カナダってこんなとこ！

日本の約 27 倍もの総面積をもつ、世界で 2 番目に広い国、カナダ。国土の 54% は森林で、農業に適した肥沃な平野、ロッキー山脈などの山岳地帯、北極圏のツンドラなど多様な地形が、10 の州と 3 の準州にわかれています。日本の 1/3 弱ほどの人口の半数以上が、五大湖とセント・ローレンス川沿い、すなわち首都オタワのあるオンタリオ州やケベック州に暮らし、残りの人もほとんどが米国との国境から 200km 以内に住んでいます。同じ国の中でも時間帯が 6 つにわかれ、オンタリオ州・ケベック州と日本との時差は 14 時間。緯度は北海道の最北端より北で、冬の寒さはきびしく、モントリオールでは－ 15℃ほどまで冷え込むことも。

カナダの建国は 1867 年。比較的新しいこの国では、多文化主義が憲法で守られ、先住民も含めて 200 以上もの民族が暮らしています。3/4 はヨーロッパ系白人ですが、アジア系も多く、カナダの人口の 18% ぐらいを示しています。在留日本人は約 7 万人。公用語は英語とフランス語で、政府は両方の普及を促進しています。

ラサール領事のなごや日記

01 名古屋は日本で一番人気のない街？

「日本で一番人気のない街へようこそ」それが河村たかし市長の第一声でした。2016年の夏に名古屋のカナダ領事に赴任して、最初にお会いした政治家が河村市長です。

スタッフから、彼については“カラフル・ポリティシャン”であるときいていました。“カラフル”は多くの意味をもちますが、私の解釈では独特の個性をもつユニークな人を連想します。河村市長はまさに個性的な人柄で、彼の装(よそお)いもまたカラフルでした。私は公務員で、ある程度の制約があるものですから、自分の着たいものを選べる自由を少しうらやましく思います。

着任して最初の家族旅行は大阪でした。今や大阪名物といえば、ユニバーサル・スタジオ・ジャパン（USJ）でしょう。オープンした2001年、私は日本に住んでいて、大規模なオープニングをはっきりと覚えています。2年目に不祥事があいつぎ、業績は低迷していったのですが、今は見事に挽回(ばんかい)をはたしました。その理由のひとつは、ハリー・ポッターのパビリオンでしょう。そして成功の要因は、ポッターの魔法だけではないと思います。

私たちがUSJを訪れたのは平日だったにもかかわらず、人気のアトラクションは長蛇(ちょうだ)の列。待つのが苦手な私は、ヒマつぶしに人間観察をしはじめました。よく見ると、あっちもこっちも、外国人ばかりではあり

河村市長との
初めての対談。
小さな記念品を交換

With Mayor Kawamura
after our first meeting.
We exchanged
small gifts

ませんか。夕方の道頓堀も同じで、いたる所に外国人観光客。

私が日本に住んでいた1990年代には、日本でこれほど多くの外国人を見ませんでした。それが、中国、韓国、東南アジアから、年間何百万人もの外国人が日本へ旅行できる時代となり、アジアの経済成長を大阪で実感したのです。2016年の訪日外国人旅行者は2千万人を突破し、東京オリンピック開催の2020年には4千万人が目標ということ。ワオ～！いうまでもなく、観光業は日本の主要産業なのです。

名古屋はどうでしょう。日本の人気観光地の調査では最下位にあると、河村市長は苦笑いしながらも、精力的に名古屋の発展を考えています。名古屋にはまだ可能性がある。私もいくつかアイデアがあるのですが、それはまたのちほど。

ラサール領事のおまけ話

カナダで大きな都市といえば？

名古屋は日本で3番目に大きな都市ですが、カナダで人口の多い都市はどこかご存じですか？1位はトロントで590万人、2位は私の故郷・モントリオールで410万人、3位がバンクーバー（250万人）、4位は88年の冬季オリンピックでフィギュアスケートの伊藤みどり選手が活躍したカルガリー（140万人）、5位は首都オタワを含むオタワ・ガティノー地域（130万人）です。（2016年しらべ）

01 Nagoya, Japan's least popular city?

"Welcome to Japan's least popular city" those were Nagoya mayor Takashi Kawamura's first words. Mayor Kawamura was the first politician I met with after the start of my posting as Canadian Consul in Nagoya in the summer of 2016.

My staff had told me he was a "colorful politician". Colorful can have many meanings but in my mind, it brings up the image of someone unique, with a strong personality. Mayor Kawamura turned out to be a "colorful" person and I noticed his clothing was also very "colorful". I was a bit envious of the freedom he enjoys in terms of dress code – as a bureaucrat I'm not allowed much freedom to be creative with my appearance...

On our first family trip after the start of my posting, we went to Osaka. Nowadays, when people think of travelling to Osaka, Universal Studios Japan (USJ) is one of the first destinations that comes to mind. When the park opened in 2001, I was still living in Japan and I clearly remember all the hoopla surrounding the grand opening. I also remember that over the next few years, the park struggled somewhat. But 15 years later, USJ had turned the corner and was visibly doing very well. One of the reasons for the turn-around was the addition of a Harry Potter pavilion. But Harry potter magic wasn't the only reason for the success of the park...

Even though we'd chosen to travel on a week day, the park was crowded and the lineups were very long, especially for the popular rides. I don't care much for waiting so I decided to do some "people watching" to kill time. I noticed that quite a few of the faces weren't Japanese. I looked around and it seemed like half of the crowd was foreign. We'd have a similar experience in Dotonbori that evening where it seemed that most of the crowd were foreign tourists.

When I first lived in Japan in the 90s there weren't as many foreigners. But now, in Osaka, I could witness the result of Asia's growing affluence, an affluence that was making it possible for millions of Chinese, Korean, Taiwanese and even Southeast Asian families to travel to Japan. In 2016, Japan had reached a new milestone with 20 million foreign visitors and Japan's target for the 2020 Tokyo Olympics was set at 40 million entries. Wow! That's when it hit me: tourism had become a major industry in Japan.

What about Nagoya? Well, Nagoya had finished dead last in a survey of popular destinations in Japan and although Kawamura was laughing about it, he was busy trying to grow Nagoya's share of tourism dollars. Personally, I think that Nagoya has a lot to offer. I have a few ideas that I'll share with you later...

By the way...

Do you know the five largest metropolitan areas in Japan and Canada?

1. Kanto (Tokyo and surroundings) 37.3 Million Metro Toronto: 5.9 Million
2. Keihanshin (Osaka and surroundings): 19.3 Million Metro Montreal: 4.1 Million
3. Chukyo (Nagoya and surroundings):9.4 million Metro Vancouver: 2.5 Million
4. Kitakyushu-Fukuoka: 5.5 million Metro Calgary: 1.4 Million
5. Shizuoka-Hamamatsu:2.8 million (census of 2015) Metro Ottawa-Gatineau: 1.3 million

02 カナダ領事、内山田洋とクールファイブを歌う

私がカラオケで披露(ひろう)する曲の半分以上は日本の歌です。ウケねらいもあるのですが、才能のなさでご迷惑をおかけすることも…。先日、日本企業の社長のお誘いでひさしぶりにカラオケへ。歌いながら、私の学生時代がよみがえってきました。

私と日本との出会いは1992年にさかのぼります。当時、モントリオール大で東アジア研究を専攻していた私は、日本語がそれまでに学んだ欧州の言語と大きく異なることを知り、きわめるには本場にいくしかないと留学を決意。そんな私に、同大で日本語を教えてくださった金谷先生が、1本のカセットテープをくれました。「ラサール君、日本にいったらカラオケにいくことがあるだろうから、いくつか練習しておくといい。よろこばれるはずだよ」と、歌詞カードまで作ってくれました。聞いてみると、ジャズっぽいサックスの音色が流れてきます。ワーオ、クール！私は熱心に練習しました。

94年に来日し、南山大で留学生活がはじまり、ついにカラオケにいく機会が訪れました。日本人は尾崎豊の「卒業」や藤井フミヤの「TRUE LOVE」などを選曲し、一方、留学生は英語のヒット曲を次々と歌い、日本人から「英語の発音、うまい！」と称賛(しょうさん)の声があがりました（あたりまえですが）。

そして、いよいよ私の番です。マイクをにぎりしめ、渋い顔で歌い

南山大学の留学生たち。私は後ろの列の左から３番目にいます

A group of Nanzan students around 1994-95. I'm right in the middle

はじめます。「あなたひとりに〜、かけ〜た〜恋〜、愛の言葉を〜信じたの〜」。内山田洋とクールファイブの「長崎は今日も雨だった」です。69年の歌でバリバリのビンテージもの。金谷先生のいわれたとおり、よろこんでもらえました…が、少し刺激が強すぎたようでした。

それからは少しだけ時代にあわせた曲（長渕剛や布袋寅泰など）も覚えました。それでも私の十八番（おはこ）は、いまも「長崎は今日も雨だった」です。時代が変わっても、いい歌は心に染みますね。もし、一緒にカラオケにいく機会がありましたら、まずは山本譲二の「みちのくひとり旅」から…。

ラサール領事のおまけ話

日本で初めて買ったCD

94年に来日して買ったCDは、こんなラインナップでした。どれもまだ手元にありますし、「巡恋歌」は今でもカラオケのレパートリーに入っています。

THE BOOM「帰ろうかな」／長渕剛「巡恋歌」／布袋寅泰「POISON」／ウルフルズ「ガッツだぜ !!」／奥田民生「息子」

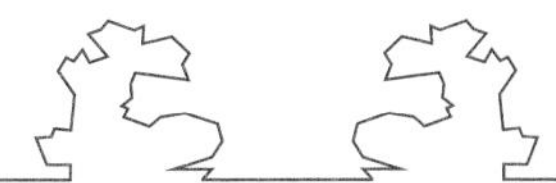

02 The Canadian Consul sings Hiroshi Uchiyamada and Cool Five

When I go to karaoke in Japan, over half of the songs I sing are in Japanese. I do that in part to try to please my hosts but my lack of talent means I end up being more of a nuisance... The other day, for the first time in many years, I was invited by a Japanese business acquaintance to an evening of karaoke. As I was singing the evening away, I started reminiscing about my college days.

My first encounter with Japan goes all the way back to 1992. At the time, as a student at the University of Montreal's Eastern Asian Studies department, I quickly discovered that Japanese was very different from all the other languages I had studied before; therefore, in order to master Japanese, I really had no choice, I had to go to Japan. That's about the time when one of my Japanese teachers at the University of Montreal approached me and handed me a cassette tape: "La Salle kun, when you go to Japan, you'll probably get invited to go to karaoke. Learn a few Japanese songs. I guarantee your hosts will get a kick out of it". Kanaya sensei also went through the trouble of printing out the lyrics to the songs on the tape. Later, when I played it at home, the room filled with the sounds of a very jazzy saxophone. How cool! I quickly started to practice and practice that song.

In 1994, I came to Japan for the first time as a foreign student to attend Nanzan University and sure enough, it wasn't long before

I was invited to join a group of friends for an evening of karaoke. The Japanese students were singing Yutaka Ozaki's "Sotsugyo (Graduation)" or Fumiya Fujii's "True Love" while the foreign students would sing hit songs in English - earning them the praise of their Japanese hosts "Wow, your English sounds so natural" (what did you expect?)

And that moment finally came, my karaoke debut in Japan. I grabbed the mic, put on my best "crooner" face and sang away: "Anata hitori ni, kakeeeta koi... Ai no kotoba o, shin-jitano..." You guessed it, that's Hiroshi Uchiyamada and Cool Five's "Nagasaki wa kyou mo ame datta (I Met a Rainy Day Again in Nagasaki)". It doesn't get more vintage than this 1969 song. Just as Kanaya sensei had predicted, my hosts were clearly impressed. But then again maybe they were also in shock...

Later, I learned a few more songs that were a better fit with the times like Tsuyoshi Nagabuchi and Tomoyasu Hotei songs (it was the 90s). But even now, "Nagasaki wa kyou mo ame datta" is still my "go to" song when I'm in a karaoke bar in Japan. No matter how old the song is, if it's a good song, it will resonate with people. Speaking of which, if we ever end up going to karaoke together, I think I'll start the evening by singing "Michinoku hitori tabi (Michinoku Lonely Trip)"...

By the way...

Buying music in Japan

Here are the first mini discs I bought in Japan in 1994. I still have them somewhere at home. "Junrenka" is still in my Karaoke repertoire today !

The Boom "Kaerokana" / Tsuyoshi Nagabuchi "Junrenka" /
Tomoyasu Hotei "Poison" / Urufuls "Guts daze" / Tamio Okuda "Musuko"

03 領事の子どもの日本名

私が大学で東アジア研究を専攻し、はじめて日本語を学ぶことになったのは20年以上も前になります。最初に習ったのは、ひらがなではなく、カタカナでした。日常生活に頻繁(ひんぱん)に使われる外来語を表すカタカナは、外国人にとって、とっかかりやすいのです。

最初の授業でカタカナ表から文字をひろい、自分の名前を書くのですが、伸ばす文字「ー」を知らない私は名字 La Salle を「ラサル」と書いたのです。先生は「あなたの名字ラサールは日本に存在していますよ」と教えてくれました。みなさんは鹿児島の有名な高校の名前をご存じですよね。そのおかげで、日本では私の名字はすぐに覚えてもらえま

領事の子どもたち
(領事の左から＝
長女さくら、次女ももこ、
長男太朗)

The Canadian consul's kids have Japanese names

した。

名前のChénier（シェニエ）についてですが、アンドレ・シェニエ、シルヴィー・シェニエのようにフランス語圏では名字としてよく使われます。しかし私の父は、とてもユニークな性格で、名前として私につけたのです。ただ曖昧（あいまい）な名前のせいで、あとあとみんなに混乱をまきおこす原因にもなったのですが…。

そういうこともあり、私の子どもにはクラシックで覚えやすい名前をと、両親のごく普通の名前をとって、長女はミシェル（フランス語版のMichelle）、長男はジャン（同じくJohn）にしました。しかし2009年生まれの次女の名前には少し悩みました。結局「エルサ」という、当時としては少し古くさい名前を選びました。でも、なんという偶然！2013年に日本でも大ヒットした「アナ雪」で雪の女王“エルサ”が登場したではありませんか。ディズニー映画の大ファンの次女は、自分の名前をとてもよろこんでくれることになったのでした。

日本とカナダの国籍をもつうちの子どもたちは、日本語の名前、「さくら」、「太朗」、「ももこ」も持っています。クラシックで世代を選ばず覚えやすいですよね。現代の日本ではかえってめずらしいかもしれませんが、最近では3人は、そちらのほうを好んで使っています。

ラサール領事のおまけ話

カナダの名づけランキング（2018）

男の子　**1. リアム　2. ジャクソン　3. ノア　4. ルーカス　5. ローガン**

女の子　**1. アヴァ　2. ミア　3. アイヴィー　4. ゾーイ　5. エヴァ**

私が生まれた1968年ごろ人気の名前は、男の子はマイケル、デイヴィッド、ジョン、女の子はリサ、ミシェル、キンバリーでした。

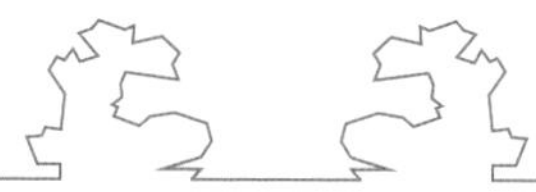

03 The Japanese names of the Canadian Consul's kids

Over 25 years have passed since I decided to major in Eastern Asian studies in college and started learning Japanese. The first thing we learned in Japanese class wasn't hiragana but rather katakana. Since loan words written in katakana are very common in Japanese and since most come from English, they are easy for foreign students to learn.

During our first class, the teacher gave us a table containing katakana characters. He then invited us to use them to write down our name in Japanese. Since I didn't know about the katakana character that stretches the vowel "ー", I wrote my family name「ラサル」without it. My teacher saw this and told me: "Your name is written「ラサール」and it already exists in Japan". Readers might be familiar with the famous high school in Kagoshima called "La Salle High School". Thanks to this lucky coincidence, my name is easy for Japanese people to remember.

My first name Chénier is relatively common in the French-speaking world (opera fans might have heard of André Chénier) and it's normally a family name. However, my father, who was a bit of an eccentric, gave it to me as a first name so it's often a source of confusion in my home country when I introduce myself.

When it came to my own children, I thought I'd spare them problems and chose more "traditional" easy-to-remember names, so we went with my parents names: we named our first daughter Michèle (French for Michelle) and named our son Jean (French equivalent of John). For our third child, a girl born in 2009, we went with Elsa, which had somewhat of an older feel to it when we chose it. But, just a few years later in 2013, the Disney movie "Frozen" comes out and what do you know, the main character, the Queen of Arendelle, is named "Elsa". Our little one is a big fan of Disney movies, so she's very pleased with her name.

Since our kids are also Japanese, they also have Japanese names: our eldest is Sakura, our son is Taro and the little one is Momoko. I'm sure you'll agree that these are all fairly "classic" and easy-to-remember names. It kinda goes against the trend right now in Japan, but interestingly, all three of our kids generally go by their Japanese first names.

By the way...

The most popular first names for boys and girls in Japan (2019)

According to the Meiji Yasuda Life Insurance Company,

Boys **1.Haruto 2.Sota 3.Minato 4.Yuto 5.Riku**

Girls **1.Mei 2.Himari 3.Hana 4.Rin 5.Sakura**

In late 60s, the most popular names for boys were Kenichi, Makoto and Takeshi and for girls it was Naomi, Yumiko and Mayumi.

04 カナダ領事は歩いて通勤

私たち家族は約４年ごとに引っ越しをしてきました。特に国境を越えるとなると、それはもう大変。その中でも、まず第一に考えなくてはならないのが、移動手段です。

以前住んでいたテキサス州ヒューストンは、全米の都市人口第４位の大都市。どこへいくにも車がないと不便でしたので、私と妻と１台ずつ車を購入しました。カナダのオタワではバスが普及しているので、家族に車１台で不自由はありませんでした。

2016年から名古屋に再び住むことになり、私たち家族が最初に手に入れたのは自転車でした。名古屋は徒歩圏内に駅、スーパー、コンビニ、歯医者、病院があり、北米とくらべてどこへいくにも便利です。

しかし数カ月後、ちょっとむずかしく感じてきました。妻の毎日の買いもの（５人家族ですよ！）や、瀬戸の両親を訪れることも車なしでは不便ですので、やはり妻に車があったほうがいいという結論に。

ちょうどそのとき、親戚のおじから８年間で58,000kmしか乗っていないダイハツ製の小型車を、破格の20万円でゲット（おじさん、本当に感謝してますよ！）。この走行距離は、カナダではなかなかありません。１年で15,000km走るのが普通です。カナダに住んでいたころ、私たちの100,000kmの車を日本の義理の父は「あんなの大丈夫か」と相当心配していました。

領事の
ファミリーカー

The Canadian Consul's
humble car

ちなみに、私の家から駅までは1.5kmで、地下鉄に乗りオフィスまでは約１時間。日本の猛暑を考えると、車のほうが快適なのですが、ふだんまったく運動をしない私に車は必要ないと、妻からはOKサインは出ず。

外国の領事というと、運転手つきの黒塗りの高級車を思い浮かべるのかもしれませんが、私は地下鉄、電車、必要に応じてタクシー。そしてうちのは小さな国産の中古車で、ほぼ妻が運転するのみ。最初はいい運動になるというぐらいの気持ちでしたが、名古屋の道から私の車１台減ることで、環境にちょっとした貢献をしているなと、満足です。カナダ領事は、今日も地下鉄に乗り、歩いて通勤。

ラサール領事のおまけ話

カナダの自動車売り上げランキング（2018）

日本車の人気が高いのがわかりますね！

1. ホンダ・シビック　2. トヨタ・カローラ　3. ヒュンダイ・エラントラ　4. マツダ3　5. シボレー・クルーズ　6. フォルクスワーゲン・ゴルフ　7. フォルクスワーゲン・ジェッタ　8. トヨタ・カムリ　9. キア・フォルテ　10. ホンダ・アコード

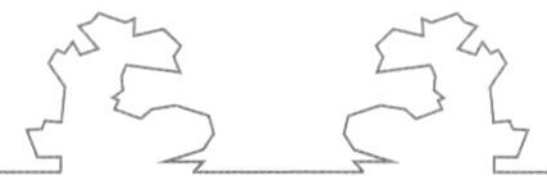

04 The Canadian Consul walks to work

Our family moves every 4 years. When the move involves crossing borders, it can be very challenging. One of the first things to consider when moving to a new city is how to get around.

Our family lived in Houston, Texas a few years back. Houston is America's 4th largest metropolitan area in terms of population. Moving around in Houston is hard without a car, so both my wife and I ended up getting one. Back home in Ottawa, the public transportation network is solid so our family could get by with just one car.

In 2016, when we moved back to Nagoya, the first "set of wheels" we got were bicycles. In Nagoya, subway stations, supermarkets, conveniences stores, dentists, hospitals are all generally within walking distance from any home, so getting around is much easier than in North America.

But a few months later, it became clear that bicycles alone just wouldn't be enough. The daily trips to the supermarket (we are a family of 5!) and the visits to the in-laws in Seto were all just too much, so we decided to get a car for my wife.

And we were in luck! One of my wife's uncles had an 8-year-old Daihatsu with only 58,000km on it and he gave us a great deal, just 200,000 yen (equals to about 2,500 Canadian dollars. Big thank you to the family!). Cars with such low mileage are pretty rare in Canada

where it's not unusual for vehicles to travel over 15,000km a year. When we were living in Canada, I remember telling my father in law in Japan that we were driving in a car with over 100,000km on it which seemed to worry him. "Are you sure that's safe?" he asked.

By the way, our house is about 1.5km from the nearest subway station and with the subway ride and the short walk to the office, my commute adds up to about one hour. On a scorching Japanese summer day, you'd think it might be a good idea to drive to work but my wife, who knows I don't get much exercise beyond my walk to work, nixed the idea of us getting a 2nd car.

When people think of a "consul" they probably think of a black chauffeur driven luxury car. But for this consul (me), it's subways, trains and occasionally taxis. The family does have a car but it's a small domestic car that my wife gets to use (almost) exclusively. At first that whole walking to work thing was just about getting a bit of exercise but when I think of it, I'm kinda glad that I'm taking one car off Nagoya streets and doing my small part for the environment. And today, yet again, the Canadian Consul takes the subway and walks to his office.

By the way...

The best-selling cars in Canada (2018)

You'll recognize many of the names. Canadians love Japanese cars!

1.Honda Civic 2.Toyota Corolla 3.Hyundai Elantra 4.Mazda 3 5.Chevrolet Cruze 6.Volkswagen Golf 7.Volkswagen Jetta 8.Toyota Camry 9.Kia Forte 10.Honda Accord

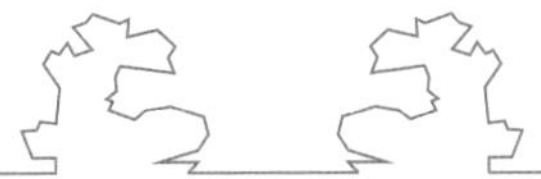

05 カナダ領事、PTA役員をつとめて

日本に赴任するにあたって、親としての第一の課題は、子どもたちの学校でした。

子どもたちはカナダ、アメリカでも週末の日本語補習校に通っていたので、私は「近所の学校でもいいんじゃない？」と安易に提案しました。妻は私ほど楽観的ではなく「それは意外とむずかしいよ」と反論。末の7歳の娘はともかく、海外で育った17歳の長女と14歳の長男には、年齢的に大学、高校受験のレースに参加するにはハードルが高すぎるとわかり、悩んだ結果、インターナショナルスクール（名古屋国際学園）を選びました。実は、子どもたちはフランス語で教育をうけていたのですが、名古屋にはフレンチスクールがなく、英語教育に切り替わったこと自体、大きな変化でありました。

インターナショナルスクールでカナダ色に装ったももこ。子どもたちは自分の出身国を祝います

Momoko in Canadian colors at the international school. The kids were celebrating their own heritage

私はPTA役員として、新学期の会議に出席した際、生徒数がここ2、3年で約150人増加し、2017年には全体で500人に達する見込みであると知りました。このままでは学校は手狭（てぜま）になり、校舎を拡張するために莫大な資金が必要になります。

この急増、もしかして名古屋周辺で開発されている三菱リージョナルジェット（MRJ）と関連し、海外からエンジニアが集中している一時的な波なのではないか、と私はちょっと心配でした。いったん計画事業が終了すれば、家族全員祖国に帰り、生徒数が縮小するだろうと。増加の波が一時的なものなら、わざわざ高いコストを払って学校を拡張すべきではない。しかし、理事長からの資料は、生徒数の増加の根源は、航空機産業だけでなくさまざまな企業にあることを統計的に示していました。

なるほど。学校は成長しているのです。それは、外国からの才能をうけいれる都市と地域の発展をも示しているのです。健全なインターナショナルスクールは、地域経済の将来にとってよい前兆です。わが“インターナショナルファミリー”にとって、すばらしい時期に名古屋に住んでいます。

ラサール領事のおまけ話

カナダのトップ大学5校

英国のTimes Higher Educations誌によると、
1. トロント大学　2. ブリティッシュ・コロンビア大学　3. マギル大学　4. マックマスター大学　5. モントリオール大学（私が日本語を学んだ大学！）でした。
ただしこのランキングは、「東大」や「京大」がトップを占める日本の大学ランキングとはちがいます。カナダのトップ官僚や医者、科学者は他の大学からも多く出ていて、トップ15校くらいまではどれもとてもいい大学です。

05 The Canadian Consul on the school's board of trustees

Our family's first priority when planning our move to Japan was finding the right school for our kids.

Our kids had always attended the weekend "hoshuko" (supplementary Japanese school) when we lived in Canada and the US, so when my wife and I discussed the options, I said naively "maybe they can attend the neighborhood school?" My wife, who did not share my optimism, reminded me that it would be really hard on the kids. That might work for our little one, who is just 7, but for our 17-year-old daughter and 14-year-old son, who were both raised abroad, entering Japan's ultra competitive university exam race so late in the game would put them at a disadvantage. After thinking it through, we opted for the Nagoya International School. Complicating things even further was the fact that until that point, our kids had always attended school in French but since there were no French options in Nagoya, the kids would have to deal with a switch to English – not an easy task.

When I sat on the school board at the start of the semester, I learned that over the last 2 or 3 years, the school's total enrollment had increased by 150 students and was expected to reach 500 students by 2017. The school was simply too small for that many students and funding for an expensive expansion had become

necessary.

My first thoughts were that this sudden increase was possibly the result of an influx of foreign engineers brought in to support Mitsubishi's MRJ program. I worried that after their job is done, this wave of families would pack up their bags and go back to their home countries, reducing enrollment considerably. If the increase is temporary, why spend so much money for an expansion? The head of the board reassured me with data showing that the increase wasn't based only on increased activity in the aerospace industry but also in other sectors.

I get it, the school is growing! And the region and city that were hosting all this international talent, were growing as well! A healthy international school truly is a good harbinger of a region's economic future. Our "international family" is very lucky to be in Nagoya during these exciting times.

By the way...

Top 5 universities in Japan

According to the Times Higher Education ranking of 2020,

1.University of Tokyo 2.Kyoto University 3.Tohoku University 4.Tokyo Institute of Technology 5.Nagoya University

"Todai" (University of Tokyo) and "Kyodai" (Kyoto University) are especially renowned elite universities in Japan. Unlike Japan, many of Canada's top doctors, scientists and bureaucrats are graduates of universities that are not in the top 5.

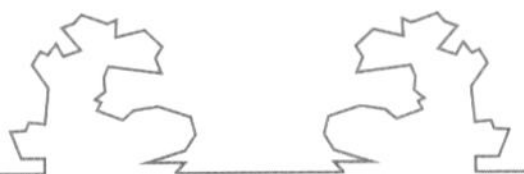

06 カナダ領事のクリスマス

1970年代のモントリオールでの子ども時代、クリスマスはいつも家族の行事でした。イブには両親、弟と真夜中にミサにいき、家では美しく包まれたプレゼントを開けるのです。ミートパイと“ブッシュ・ド・ノエル”とよばれる伝統的なケーキを食べる、フランス系カナディアン式のクリスマスディナーをささやかにいただくのがイブのすごし方でした。翌日のクリスマスは、盛大な家族のお祝いです。父は9人兄弟の長男で、祖父母、おじさん、おばさんの配偶者といとこもいるので、30人以上が集まりにぎやかでした。

私が名古屋に住んでいた90年代、12月になると街はクリスマスらしい風景となり、やはり日本でもクリスマスを祝うことを知りました。テレビをつけると、フライドチキンのクリスマスバレルがおいしそうに映し出され、ラジオからは山下達郎さんの「クリスマス・イブ」が聞こえてきました。同時に、日本では家族だけでなく、特に若いカップルに支持されていることに気づきました。カナダよりももっとロマンチックですね。日本は外国の文化をとりいれ、工夫しながら独自のものにするのが本当に上手です。

しかし、97年のクリスマスが私にとって人生最大のロマンチックなイベントになりました。というのは、その年に結婚することになったのです！正式な教会での式は半年後にカナダで行いましたが、12月24日

日本で結婚式を
あげた数カ月後、
カナダであげた結婚式の写真

A picture from our wedding ceremony held in Canada a few months after we got married in Japan

にふたりで春日井市役所へ婚姻届を出しにいきました。

20年以上、楽しいときも苦しいときも、ずっと一緒に歩んできてくれて本当に感謝しています。あなたとの結婚は私の人生最高の決断でした。これからのふたりの20年を夢見つつ。

Je t'aime beaucoup, Noriko（愛してるよ、紀ちゃん）！

ラサール領事のおまけ話

フランス系カナディアン式のクリスマスディナー

フレンチカナディアンのクリスマスでは､「トゥルティエール」と呼ばれるミートパイにビーフシチューと七面鳥の丸焼きをいただくのが一般的です。デザートには、丸太の形をしたフランスの伝統的なケーキ「ブッシュ・ド・ノエル」。故郷で家族とすごした冬のホリデーを、とてもなつかしく感じます。

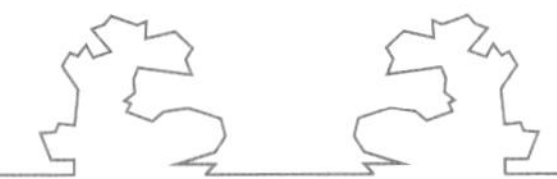

06 The Canadian Consul's Christmas

As a child in Montreal in the 1970s, Christmas was always a family affair. On Christmas Eve, my parents, brother and I would go to midnight mass and then come home to open all our beautifully wrapped Christmas presents. For dinner, it was a traditional French-Canadian Christmas meal: meat pie and "bûche de Noel". On Christmas Day, December 25, the family would celebrate again but on a bigger scale. My father was the eldest of 9 kids, so when the extended family got together – the grandparents, the uncles, the aunts and their spouses and cousins – it added up to well over 30 people!

When I first lived in Nagoya in the 90s, I noticed that come December, the city would dress up in Christmas colors and it dawned on me that Japan celebrates Christmas as well. When you turned on the TV, there was Christmas themed advertising offering KFC's Christmas barrel. Tune in the radio and Christmas themed songs like Tatsuro Yamashita's "Christmas Eve" filled the air. But I also noticed that the Japanese version of Christmas was a favorite not just with families but with young couples. Christmas in Japan was definitely more "romantic" than in Canada. Japan is very good at adopting foreign traditions but often gives them its own Japanese twist.

However, little did I know that an event in my life would give

Christmas an even more romantic meaning: I got married to my wife Noriko exactly 20 years ago, on Christmas Eve, 1997! The Church ceremony would take place about 6 months later in Canada, but on December 24, 1997, Noriko and I went to Kasugai City Hall to sign the papers that made us a married couple.

Thank you Noriko for being by my side for over 20 years, through the good times and the bad. I'm truly grateful. Marrying you was the best decision I ever made. I'm sure the next 20 years will be even better!

Je t'aime beaucoup, Noriko ! (I love you Noriko!)

By the way...

Christmas is not a holiday in Japan

Christmas is celebrated in many ways in Japan, in music, on TV, in stores, even Christmas cakes sell very well in Japan! But Christmas day, December 25, is still a regular working day. That took some getting used to when I first lived here back in the 90s. Christmas is such a big thing in most western countries that it felt odd to see everybody going about their daily lives like it's a normal day. But when you think of it, that's just normal. It must be strange for Japanese people not to have Golden Week or Obon holidays when they live in foreign countries.

07 領事の妻は“花よりケーキ”

バレンタインデーも日本とカナダでは、ちがいます。90年代、名古屋で英語教師をしていたとき、私もいくつかチョコレートをもらいました。最初は少しおどろいたのですが、日本には日ごろの感謝をあらわす義理（ぎり）チョコという文化があるのを知り、甘い物好きの私は大歓迎でした。

カナダでは、バレンタインデーは、カップルのためのイベントです。男性と女性の両方が、おたがいに贈り物をします。日本では、女性からの「告白」の意味をもつようですね。最近では、カナダでも若者の間で少しだけコクハクの意味をもつことがあるようです。店には、やっぱり、チョコレートやピンクのカードがならびます。子どもたちはキャンディーをつけたカードを配りあいます。

2004年に日本を去って私たち家族がカナダへ移住したとき、長女は５歳で日本語しか話せませんでした。日本の祖父におりがみを送ってもらい、妻と娘はハートの形におり、メッセージのかわりに、カタカナでクラスメートひとりひとりの名前を書いたものをわたしていました。その娘もティーンエイジャーになると、男の子から花束をもらってくるようになりました。

花といえば、私が若いときに、父からくりかえし言われたことを思い出します。それは、“息子よ、花の力を過小評価するなよ”。父によれ

ば、恋愛成就の秘訣は花だそうです。私は人生の先輩からの教えを忠実に守り、ことあるごとに女性（たち）に花を贈りました。父からの教訓は成功することもあれば、そうでないこともある、としておきましょう。

妻と結婚する前、毎週土曜日のデートに、私は当時住んでいた今池の、アパート近くの花屋さんで小さな花束を買い、プレゼントしていました。３、４カ月がすぎたころ、妻が「ありがとう。けど花はもういらない。どうせなら、ケーキのほうがいい」。ふだんケーキなど買ったことがない私のために、わかりやすいように「モンブランね」と指定までしてくれました。あれから20年。私は３月のホワイトデーに、名古屋でとびきりおいしい「告白」のモンブランをさがしています。

ラサール領事のおまけ話

巨額のバラが輸入されるカナダのバレンタイン

カナダではさまざまな花が生産されていますが、バレンタインデーのころ、花屋の店先にならぶバラの花は、ほとんどが輸入品。2016年には、7170万ドル（約78億円！）相当ものバラが、主にコロンビアとエクアドルからカナダへ輸入されています。
（出典：カナダ国際貿易データベース）

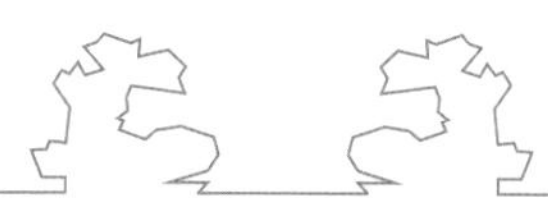

07 The Consul's wife prefers cakes to flowers

Valentine's Day is celebrated differently in Canada and Japan. Back in the 90s when I was an English teacher here, I remember receiving chocolates now and then. I was surprised at first but I learned about the Japanese custom of offering "giri choco" (literally "duty" chocolate) as a 'thank you' to friends and colleagues. I love sweets so this was a welcome tradition.

In Canada, Valentine's Day is mainly for couples and both women and men give each other presents. In Japan, when a woman offers a gift, it can also become a "declaration of love". In Canada as well, especially among the younger crowd, gifts can be used to send "messages" and when Valentine's Day comes around, store shelves are stocked full of pink cards and chocolates. Smaller kids also get in on the fun and offer each other cards in which they sometimes insert a piece of candy.

In 2004, when our family left Japan and settled in Canada, our eldest daughter was 5 years old and spoke only Japanese. Her grandfather in Japan sent her some origami paper and with her mother's help, she folded them into the shape of hearts, one for each of her classmates. On each heart, she wrote their names in katakana before handing them out on Valentine's Day at school. Our eldest daughter is now a teenager, an age when girls sometimes receive

flowers as present.

Speaking of flowers, I remember something my father told me repeatedly when I was young. "Son, never underestimate the power of flowers". According to Dad, flowers were a powerful secret weapon of seduction. I took my dad's advice and the tradition was passed on to me. And I would go on to offer flowers to my love interests during my youth – with mixed results. Let's keep it at that.

Before we got married, Noriko and I would go on dates every Saturday. I lived in Imaike at the time and there was a small flower shop near my apartment where I would pick out a bouquet of flowers that I would hand Noriko every time we met. This went on for 3 or 4 months until my wife said, "Thank you. I think I've had enough flowers. But you could buy me cakes instead" and in case I didn't know what to buy, she added, "I like Mont Blancs". 20 years have passed... This year again, I'm looking for the best "declaration of love" Mont Blanc in Nagoya to offer my wife on White Day in March.

By the way...

Chocolate rage in Japan

In Japan, on February 14, women give chocolates to men while on "White Day" March 14th, men return the favor. About 500 billion yen's worth ($4.5 billion) of chocolate is purchased in Japan around those dates!

08 カナダ領事、コンビニの変化に思う

私がつとめるカナダ領事館は地下鉄の久屋大通駅で降り、徒歩５分のところにあります。そのわずか５分圏内に４軒のコンビニエンスストアがあります。20年前、私が留学生として名古屋に住んでいたころ、よくコンビニへおにぎりやタバコ（いまはやめました）を買いにいったものです。

４年前の８月に日本に帰ってきて、久しぶりにコンビニに入ってみると、まちがいなく昔より進化していて、ヘルシーとグルメ感が増し、高

いつも笑顔で
迎えてくれる中国出身の
店員さんと一緒に

With a Chinese employee
at Family Mart

級感（イベリコ豚の生ハムなんて）さえただよわせ、さすがだと思いました。でも、もっとおどろいたのは、支払いのときです。若い女性店員の流暢（りゅうちょう）な日本語にはわずかですが、なまりがあって、ふと名札を見ると、中国名がひらがなで記されていました。そして、よく見まわすと、他の３人の従業員も外国人。２人は中国人、１人はインド人でした。

20年前は、店員は学生か主婦、または経営者の家族だったはずです。私は興味をかきたてられ、その店員に話しかけると、彼女たちは留学生で、パートタイムでここで働いていると。いまでは彼らのように学歴が高く、日本語が堪能（たんのう）な若い外国人を、コンビニだけでなく、飲食店、アパレル店でも見かけるようになりました。

彼らはサービス業における巨匠・日本人から、貴重な経験をさせてもらって、故国に戻ったあとに、役立たせるはずです。それならきびしい労働市場と少子化をかかえている日本は、そういった若者たちをこの地にとどめる努力をするべきではないかとも思うのです。

彼らのように日本語、日本の習慣、サービス精神などを会得した人材は、将来、日本企業と中国やインドにおける文化的なギャップを解決し、両国にとってよりよい環境をつくるのに、重要な役割をはたしてくれます。彼らをうけいれ、労働市場をひろげるかは、日本が解決すべき課題です。

ラサール領事のおまけ話

カナダのコンビニ事情は…？

カナダで最も大きなコンビニチェーンは「Couche-Tard（クシュタール、フランス語で“遅くに寝る”という意味）」。世界的にコンビニ事業を展開する企業で、傘下にある「サークルK」などさまざまな商標のもと、米国、欧州、アジアのコンビニ網を運営しています。

08 The Canadian Consul and changing convenience stores

The Canadian Consulate is a 5-minute walk from Hisaya Odori station where I get off every day. In the short distance to my office, there are 4 convenience stores. 20 years ago, when I was a student in Nagoya, I would often drop by the convenience store to buy "onigiri" or cigarettes (I've quit smoking since).

I came back to Japan in August 4 years ago and soon enough, I made my first visit in many years to a Japanese convenience store. It was clear that Japanese convenience stores had improved during my absence. There were more healthy, gourmet options and a few high-end offerings to boot (Iberico pork!). That's Japan for you, I thought. However, the biggest surprise was waiting for me at the cash register. The cashier, a young lady, spoke Japanese fluently but I could detect a small accent. I looked at her nametag and saw a Chinese name written in hiragana. A quick scan with my eyes revealed that all 3 employees in the store were foreigners. Two were Chinese and the other was from India.

20 years ago, convenience store employees were generally Japanese students, middle-aged part time staff or members of the family running the store. I had a quick conversation with the young cashier and found out she was a student at a local university and was

working part-time to earn some money. Nowadays, highly educated students with a good command of the Japanese language can be found not only in convenience stores but also in restaurants and clothing stores.

These foreigners were getting great training in the service industry, from the masters of service themselves, the Japanese. I couldn't help but think that this experience would be put to good use once they returned to their country. Then again, in an aging society struggling with increasing labor shortages, shouldn't Japan be trying to keep more of these promising young adults in the country?

They speak Japanese, know the culture and understand customer expectations in terms of service. They could help bridge cultural gaps and play an important role in creating better relations between Japan and countries like India and China. Should Japan further open its doors and make it easier for foreign students to integrate the labor market? That's a question for the Japanese people to answer.

By the way...

Convenience stores in Canada

The largest convenience store operator in Canada is "Couche-Tard" (literally "sleep late"). It's one of the largest convenience store operations in the world and operates stores under many different banners including "Circle K" that they own.

09 東山線にジャイアント

それは領事館への通勤途中の地下鉄東山線でのことです。私の負けでした！　先週は２日続けて黒星…。そう、背くらべです。

私の身長は189cmで、故郷モントリオールでも高いほうです。私より高いと、「ジャイアント（巨人）」と呼んだりもしていました。

90年代に私が日本に滞在していたころ、背が高いおかげで少し得したことといえば、満員電車。通勤ラッシュ時、スーツ姿（クールビズがはやる前）で汗びっしょりのサラリーマンの中、頭ひとつ飛びぬけている私は、フレッシュな空気を吸え、視界も広いので、迷うことなく効率的に進むことができたのです。

それが、20年がたち、車内の見晴らしが少し変わりました。自分と同じくらいか、もっと高い日本人が出没するようになり、幸か不幸か仲間が増えてしまいました。

私がテキサス州、ヒューストンに赴任していたころ、日本からダルビッシュ有（ゆう）選手がメジャーリーグのテキサス・レンジャーズに入団しました。196cmの彼は、外国人選手の中でもまったくひけをとることがなく、マウンドにそびえたっていました。

予兆は感じていたのです。日本人が大きくなっていることを。最近では、193cmの期待の二刀流、大谷翔平選手ですね。そういえば、私が利用する駅では、体格のいい若者をよく見かけます。

赴任当初、一体どういうことなんだと毎朝ふしぎに思っていたら、近くにスポーツに力を入れている東邦高校があると知り、納得。スポーツの世界だけでなく、一般的な日本人の平均身長の右肩上がりの上昇は、やはり食生活の変化が大きな要因でしょうか。

私の大好物はなんといってもステーキです。私が留学生だったころは、牛肉は高くてめったに食べられませんでした。それが、最近は手軽においしい赤身のステーキを食べられるレストランが増えたことも、昔とはちがううれしい変化です。魚をよく食べる日本人がお肉もよく食べるようになったんですね。この「肉」ブームのおかげで、日本のあちこちにジャイアントを見かける日も遠くはないでしょう。

大谷翔平

A giant pitcher,
Shohei Ohtani

ラサール領事のおまけ話

カナダ出身のメジャーリーガーは？

カナダの気候では、野球ができる季節は短く、野球選手を育てるのは困難。メジャーリーグにいるカナダ出身の選手は、2018年現在、11人だけです。現役で最も有名なカナダ人メジャーリーガーはシンシナティ・レッズのジョーイ・ボットでしょう。ボットは2010年にMVPに輝き、2011年にはゴールドグラブ賞を獲得した一塁手。出塁率リーグ1位を現在までに7度獲得しています。

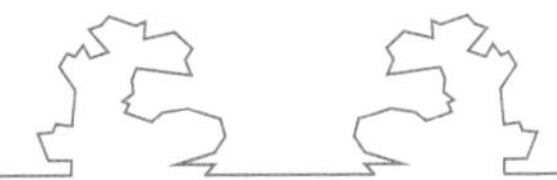

09 Giants on the Higashiyama Line

It happened again today on the Higashiyama Line, during my commute to the consulate: I "lost". I "lost" 2 days in row last week. I lost at the "who's the tallest on the subway car" game…

I'm 189cm tall which is rather tall even in my hometown of Montreal. When someone is taller than me, I call them "giants".

Back when I first lived in Japan in the 90s, one of the advantages of being tall was when riding the subway. On a rush hour subway car, surrounded, and often pressed against men sweating in their suits (this was before "cool biz" i.e. summer dress campaign in Japan encouraging people to wear lighter clothes in order to save energy), it was great to have my head above the crowd where the air was a bit "fresher". Another advantage is the view: I could see all around me, which made it easier to "plot" my route out of the car.

20 years later, my view inside the subway cars has changed somewhat and there are now more Japanese people who are just as tall and even taller than I am. Like it or not, I've got company at the top.

I happened to be in Houston, Texas on a posting, when Yu Darvish joined the Texas Rangers in the major leagues. At 196cm he was a towering figure on and off the mound.

It was an "omen" sorts, a sign that the Japanese were getting taller.

More recently, the promising multitalented Shohei Otani, at 193cm, is another great example. Speaking of which, I noticed that a surprising number of kids near the subway station I commute from were tall and athletic. So many that I found it a bit odd and wondered why. I found out that Toho High School, one of the top ranked baseball high schools in Japan, was located in the neighborhood. Mystery solved. But the phenomenon isn't limited to athletes. The average height of ordinary Japanese folks is also rising and the changing Japanese diet is likely one of the main reasons.

I just love steak but when I was a student in Japan I couldn't enjoy it very often because beef was too expensive. But nowadays, enjoying a good steak in a restaurant has become much more affordable - another welcome change from the past. Japanese people, who've always eaten a lot of fish, have also become big consumers of meat. Thanks to this "meat boom", the day when "giants" become an even more common sight on the streets of Japan is likely not too far.

By the way...

Major leaguers from Canada

The climate in Canada means the baseball season is very short which makes it hard to raise many elite baseball players. Only 11 Canadian-born athletes played in Major League games in 2018. The most famous active Canadian major leaguer is probably Joey Votto of the Cincinnati Reds. Votto was the National League MVP in 2010 and won a Gold Glove at first base in 2011. He's led the NL in OBP 7 times during his career.

10 カナダ領事、ブラックサンダーを応援する

私はスナックが大好きです。いつもきまって、ロッテや明治のミルクの板チョコを買っていました。最近順位の入れかえがあり、首位がブラックサンダーに！　よくコンビニのレジ横においてあるアレです。種類もたくさんありますが、なかでもブラックサンダー・ボルトが一番のお気にいりです。それを、これまた最近のお気にいりの飲み物・カフェラテと一緒に食べると、「セ・ボ〜ン（最高）！」。

ふと、どこの大手メーカーかと包装紙を見たら「有楽製菓株式会社」という聞いたことのないメーカー。しかも、豊橋の工場で製造しているではないですか。妻にきいてみると、やっぱり知っていました。しかも、私たちがカナダに住んでいたころ、義父が子どもたちに日本からよく送ってくれていたらしいのです。私には一度もくれなかったのに。

カナダの領事として、私の仕事のひとつは、日本からカナダへの投資促進です。カナダへ進出する企業に対し、用地や専門家の紹介などについて、全面的にサポートします。先日はある愛知県の自動車部品メーカーが新たな設備投資をする予定でしたが、私たちは法人税の影響についてアドバイスしました。愛知県からはトヨタ、デンソーなどがすでに進出しています。ブラックサンダーのように、ユニークな日本の食品メーカーは、カナダ市場でうけいれられる可能性があると思います。

外国の食品メーカーで、カナダでの事業を通じて北米全体へ拡大し

今日の愛妻弁当
（しかもかっこいいStarWars
バッグで）チキンサンドと
ミックスジュース、おやつに
はブラックサンダー。
Merci　紀ちゃん　！

My lunch in a cool
Star Wars bag.
Merci Noriko!

ている例があります。金色の包装紙で包んだ岩のようなチョコ、Rocher（ロシェ）で有名なイタリアの食品会社Ferrero（フェレロ）がそうです。パンにぬって食べる人気商品のチョコレートスプレッド、Nutella（ヌテラ）は最近では日本でも見かけますが、1980年代にカナダで販売を開始し、2006年にはカナダに工場を設立するまでに成長しました。

さっそく有楽製菓に連絡をしたところ、近いうちに会社訪問ができることになりました。彼らが国際的なビジネス展開を視野に入れているというならば、応援したいと思います。工場見学では、試食もできたりするのかなあとちょっと期待しながら。

ラサール領事のおまけ話

カナダでは英国ブランドが人気

カナダのチョコレート市場はアメリカとはずいぶん異なり、イギリス領であったことが影響してか、キャドバリーやロントリーといったイギリスのお菓子メーカーに人気があります。私はチョコレートが大好きなので、新しい国に行くたびに、その土地のチョコレートを試すのを楽しみにしています。

10 The Canadian Consul is a fan of Black Thunder

I love snacks. I'd always been partial to chocolate bars from Lotte or Meiji but recently, there's been a change at the top of my snack "hit parade" and Black Thunder is now top on the list! I'm sure you've seen it, it's that small chocolate bar that's a staple next to the cash register in convenience stores. There are many different kinds of Black Thunder but my favorite is the Volt. A nice Black Thunder with a cup of "café au lait" (my favorite drink of the moment), and mmm, "c'est si bon!"

I wondered who made this great little snack so I looked at the label and it said "Yuraku Seika". Hum, never heard of them. But hey, look at this, they make them in a plant located right here in Toyohashi, Aichi! Well, if I hadn't heard of Black Thunder, that wasn't the case for my wife. Not only that, but my wife told me that when we lived in Canada, my father-in-law would often send some Black Thunder mini bars for the kids. But no one bothered sharing with me...

One of my jobs as Canadian Consul in Nagoya is to encourage investment into Canada. When Japanese companies are interested, we help them find land or introduce service providers, we give them our full support. When an Aichi company was thinking of expanding their plant in Canada, I ended up giving them some advice on the fiscal implications. Aichi based Toyota and Denso have large

operations in Canada. I thought a company that makes a unique product like the Black Thunder chocolate bars, might also be successful in the Canadian market.

There are examples of foreign food manufacturers using Canada as a launching pad into the larger North American market. Italian Ferrero, maker of those rock-like chocolates covered in a golden aluminium foil called "Rocher", is such a company. You might have also seen their popular chocolate spread called Nutella in Japan recently. Ferrero started selling Nutella in the Canadian market in 1980 and sales grew to the point where they established a production facility there in 2006.

So I decided to contact Yuraku Seika and I'm happy to tell you that I'll be visiting them in the near future. If they have any plans for international expansion, I'll make sure to offer my support. I'll be honest, I'm also hoping for some samples coming my way during the plant tour.

By the way...

Chocolate consumption in Japan

Chocolate was first introduced in Japan in the late 18th Century. Japanese Confectionery brands like Morinaga and Meiji got their start in the Taisho Era (1912-1926). Chocolate consumption is on the rise in Japan and the average Japanese eats an average of 2.2 kg of chocolate a year, but it's still much lower than the Canadian average of 6.4 kg per capita.

11 カナダ領事、ドラゴンズを応援する

以前、中日ドラゴンズのマーケティング担当の方とお会いする機会がありました。メジャーリーガーだった松坂選手がドラゴンズとサインしたことなどを熱く語っていて、2018年のドラゴンズにとても期待がわきました。数週間後、領事館にドラゴンズのロゴつき封筒が届き、ナゴヤドームでの試合のチケットが2枚入っているではありませんか！ さて、誰と行く？

そう、お義父さんしかいません。いったん野球シーズンがスタートすると、お義父さんはテレビの前から動きません。スカパーに入っているので、全試合生中継で見られてしまうのです。義実家にはリビングにテレビが2台あり、1台はお義父さんのカープ観戦用（義父は広島出身）なのです。

ドラゴンズのユニフォームを着た強力助っ人（？）の私

Me in Dragons uniform

昔、お義父さんとでかけるときは、いつも彼の招待でした。90年代後半のことです。結婚してすぐに名古屋場所へもつれていってくれました。圧倒的に強かった貴乃花、表情豊かな武蔵丸…、力士たちを近くで見られ、ものすごく興奮したのを覚えています。

20年たったいま、やっとお義父さんを招待できる番がきました。はずかしくないように、スーツでビシッときめ、ドーム前で待ちあわせ。ドラゴンズ対ジャイアンツ戦を間近で見られる特別席。お義父さんは両方のチームの選手名はもちろん、彼らの成績や年俸まで知っているほどの野球通です。ジャイアンツの４番打者ゲレーロを指さし、「ドラゴンズで去年本塁打王をとったけど、ジャイアンツにもってかれた！」など専属解説つき。

その夜、ドラゴンズは試合に負けたものの、お義父さんは楽しんでくれたようです。思えば、私からのはじめてのお返しかも。ちっちゃいプレゼントだけど、これからちょこちょこ贈るから楽しみにしていてください。

ラサール領事のおまけ話

ラサール領事の故郷のチームは…？

カナダで人気のあるスポーツといえば、アイスホッケー。私の故郷、モントリオールは、世界で最も有名なホッケーチーム「モントリオール・カナディアンズ」の本拠地です。モントリオール・カナディアンズはナショナルホッケーリーグ（NHL）最古のチームで、1909年創設。優勝チームに与えられるスタンレー・カップをリーグ最多の24度受賞しています。

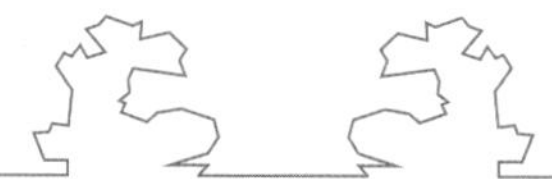

11 The Canadian Consul is a fan of the Chunichi Dragons

A while back, I was lucky enough to meet the marketing director for the Chunichi Dragons (Nagoya's professional baseball team) at a work-related event. He was all excited that the Dragons had signed former major league pitcher Matsuzaka and he had high hopes for the Dragons' 2018 season. A few weeks after our chance meeting, the Consulate received an envelope featuring the Dragons Logo. I opened it and, what do you know, two tickets to a Dragons game! Now the big question, who to take with me?

That's an easy one to answer, if you're talking baseball in our family, that can only mean "oto san". Once the baseball season starts, my father-in-law is literally glued to the TV set. He's signed up for SKY PerfecTV, so he can watch all the games live. The in-laws have got two television sets in their living room and one of them is basically reserved for watching Carp games (The Carps are a team in Hiroshima where my father-in-law is originally from)

In the past, whenever I went out with my father-in-law, he would be the one doing the inviting – it was his treat. In the late 90s, not long after I married his daughter, "oto san" took me to the Nagoya Basho sumo tournament. Back in those days, Takanohana was dominant; I also vividly remember Musashimaru and his very expressive face. I

remember how thrilling it was to be able to see these famous sumo wrestlers up close.

20 years later, it's now my turn to take "oto san" out. I wanted to make him proud so I wore a nice suit and we met near Nagoya Dome. We had great seats to see the Dragons take on the Giants. Of course, "oto san" knew all the players from both teams, and being a baseball fiend, he knew not only their names but their statistics and salary as well! Pointing at the Giants' cleanup hitter Guerrero, he said "he was a Dragon last year and the league's home run leader but the Giants lured him away"; I enjoyed the game with my own private broadcaster.

Although the Dragons ended up losing the game, it looks like "oto san" enjoyed his evening at the ballpark. Come to think of it, that might have been the first time I was returning his many favors. Oto san, it was just a small gift but you can look forward to many more!

By the way...

Baseball teams in Japan

There are 2 leagues in Japanese professional baseball, the Central League and Pacific League, and there are 6 teams in each league. In the Central League, Nagoya is home to the Dragons, Hiroshima to the Carps, Tokyo to the Swallows and Giants, Yokohama to the BayStars, and Osaka to the Tigers. In the Pacific League, there are the Chiba-based Marines, Fukuoka-based Hawks, Sapporo-based Fighters, Kansai-based Buffaloes, Saitama-based Lions and Sendai-based Golden Eagles.

12 カナダ領事の“親戚”さがし

名古屋の活気ある経済は、つねに日本全土の労働者をひきよせています。私の妻の母は岐阜、父は広島の出身ですが、名古屋で出会い、結婚し、愛知に根をおろすことになったのでした。

私がつとめる在名古屋カナダ領事館は、東海地区をおもに担当しており、そのひとつである岐阜市は、カナダのサンダーベイ市と姉妹都市です。積極的な交流活動がされており、私も何度か岐阜を訪れることがあります。彼らのイベントに招待され、スピーチをする際は、きまって義母が揖斐郡出身であることを言います。「会場の中に田代さん（義母の旧姓）はいませんか？ 親戚かもしれませんよ」と笑いをさそいます。ちなみに、妻は「田代という名字はぜんぜんめずらしくないよ」と指摘し「親戚だらけになるよ」と私の親戚さがし活動をちょっと笑っています。

そういえば La Salle という名字もカナダでは特にめずらしくありません。通っていた高校にはもうひとりの La Salle がいました。親戚ではなかったのですが、その共通点のせいで、身近に感じたものです。私にとって外国である日本では、義理の家族と同じ名字と聞いただけで、親近感を勝手にいだいてしまうのでした。

さて、義父の故郷についてですが、広島は私の担当地域外ですが、たまたまイベントで代理としてスピーチする機会がありました。もちろ

私の親戚の
川本さんたち
（写真中央が義兄夫婦と息子、
その右が義両親）

Dining out with
my Kawamoto "shinseki"
(Onisan with his baby son
and wife, mother and
father in law)

ん、広島出身の義父のことを話すことを忘れずに。「川本さんがここにいたら、親戚かもしれませんよ」もね。さらには、義父が熱烈な広島カープファンだとつけくわえて、大ウケ（あっ、中日新聞さん、すみません）。

するとイベント後に、60代の男性が、20代後半ぐらいの青い目の若者をつれてやってきました。いただいた名刺を見ると、“川本”さんではありませんか。青年は義理の息子で、私と同じフランス系カナダ人。親戚かどうか確認できませんでしたが、おもしろい偶然でした。こんな出会いがあると広島がぐっと身近に感じられますし、親戚さがし活動がやめられなくなります。

ラサール領事のおまけ話

カナダのよくある名字ベスト10

1. スミス　2. ブラウン　3. トレンブレイ　4. マーティン 5. ロイ 6. ウィルソン　7. マクドナルド　8. ギャニオン　9. ジョンソン　10. テイラー

多くの名前がイギリスやスコットランド由来ですが、トレンブレイ、ロイ、ギャニオンはフランス由来の名前です。マーティンはイギリスにもフランスにもある名前ですね。私の名前、ラサールは、上位100位以内にはありませんが、それほどめずらしくもありません。

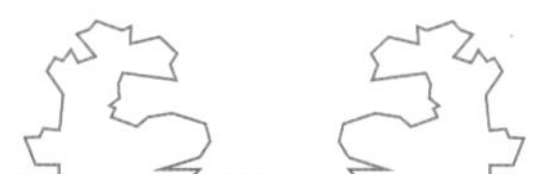

12 The Canadian Consul searches for relatives

Nagoya's dynamic economy has always attracted workers from across Japan. My wife's mother is from Gifu and her father is from Hiroshima but they met in Nagoya, married and put down roots in Aichi prefecture.

The Nagoya Consulate where I work covers the Tokai region, which of course includes Gifu city, a city that has a twinning with Canada's Thunder Bay. Gifu City and Thunder Bay have a very active twinning and I've had the chance to visit Gifu many times. When I deliver a speech in Gifu prefecture, I make sure to mention that my mother-in-law comes from Ibi district. I generally play the family card a bit more to try to get a few laughs from the audience: "Is there anybody in the room named Tashiro? (my mother-in-law's maiden name) Cause we might be related!" My wife teases me about my ongoing search for Japanese relatives. She reminded me: "Tashiro is a very common family name in Japan so you'll end up with more relatives than you can handle!"

Speaking of names, my own family name "La Salle" is not uncommon back in Canada. I remember there was another "La Salle" at my high school. He wasn't a relative, but our shared family name somehow made him feel a bit like one. Japan is a foreign country for me but when I meet people here who have the same family names as

my in-laws, I can't help but feel some kind of kinship.

My father-in-law's hometown of Hiroshima is not in an area that we cover at the Canadian Consulate in Nagoya. But I got called in as a last-minute replacement for a colleague and got an opportunity to deliver a speech in Hiroshima once. Of course, that was my chance to mention my Hiroshima father-in-law! "Is there anybody in the room named Kawamoto? We might be relatives!" I also added that my father-in-law was a hardcore fan of the Hiroshima Carps. The crowd loved it! (Apologies to the Chunichi for mentioning the Carps)

A bit later, as the event died down, a Japanese gentleman in his sixties accompanied by a young "blue-eyed" man in his twenties approached me. The older man hands me his business card and, what do you know, his name was "Kawamoto". The young man next to him was his son-in-law who, as it happens, was French-Canadian just like me! We couldn't quite confirm that we were relatives but you have to admit, it was a very interesting coincidence. Thanks to this chance encounter, Hiroshima feels closer to me now, and vindicated, my search for relatives across Japan continues!

By the way...

10 most common family Names in Japan (2018)

1.Sato 2.Suzuki 3.Takahashi 4.Tanaka 5.Watanabe
6.Ito 7.Nakamura 8.Kobayashi 9.Yamamoto 10.Kato

Tashiro and Kawamoto are not in the top 100 but they're not rare either.

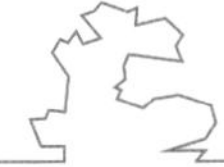

13 カナダ領事、あんかけスパを愛す

私はいったん名古屋を離れると、「名古屋のカナダ人代表」をかってでて、時には「名古屋のフードアンバサダー（大使）」の大役までつとめることがあります（ずうずうしくて、すみません）。

2017年末に、辻ウェルネスクッキングとのコラボレーションによる、カナダの食材を使ったランチレセプションが大阪で開催され、私も参加しました。私のテーブルには関西地域の食品業界のジャーナリスト5人が同席。会話は、カナダの食べ物からはじまって、名古屋めしへとうつりました。「モーニング」についても話題になりました。あるジャーナリストは、「あんかけスパ」のファンだと言いました。それで私は、あのあんかけスパが名古屋名物であることをはじめて知りました。

私が留学生だったころ、南山大近くのマンガ喫茶で食べたのがはじめてでした。「なんだ、これは？」とおどろきました。どろっとした茶色のソースとスパイシーな味。いままで食べたことのないふしぎなスパゲティでした。でもなぜだか、また食べたくなるのです。

私がいま住んでいる名東区の家から駅までの徒歩15分の間に、小さなあんかけスパ専門店があります。毎日前を通るのですが、入ったことがありませんでした。ある日、出張で帰りが遅くなるのがわかっていたので「食べて帰ったほうが、ママはラクじゃない？」と妻に聞くと「じゃあ、そうしてくれる？」。予想どおりの返答で、私は堂々とその

仕事の後のごほうび、
あんかけスパゲティ

Ankake spaghetti,
a yummy treat
after work

お店に入ったのです。

何をたのんでいいのかわからなくて「定番ください！」と言ってみると数分後、大きなお皿にのった、茶色いソースのスパゲティがやってきました。ひと口食べると、「そうそう、この味！」、25年前がよみがえってきました。私は大満足で、それからは、ちょくちょく訪れ、あんかけスパは私の出張後のごほうびとなったのでした。このおいしい名古屋名物の伝統をたやさぬよう、この本にとりあげることで、今日もまたフードアンバサダーとしての重要な任務をはたすのでした。

ラサール領事のおまけ話

カナダ人は普段何を食べる？

カナダではイタリア料理がとてもポピュラー。カナダの子どもはスパゲティやラザニアを家庭で食べて育ちます。日本食もどんどん人気を増しており、寿司店はずいぶん前からカナダでもめずらしくありません。ここ10年くらいでは、ラーメン店も人気です。

13 The Canadian Consul loves ankake spaghetti

As soon as I leave Nagoya for other Japanese cities, I instantly become a roaming "representative" not just for Canada but also for the city of Nagoya. Every now and then, I take on an even greater role and become "a food ambassador" for this great city. (Forgive my brazen behavior)

In 2017, the Consulate collaborated with the Tsuji Wellness Cooking School and held a Canadian lunch reception in Osaka that featured Canadian food. I attended the event and hosted a table of Kansai food industry journalists. The conversation started on Canadian food but eventually turned to Nagoya specialties. One of the journalists mentioned the famous "morning special" offered in Nagoya coffee shops. Another mentioned he was a fan of "ankake spaghetti". And that's when I learned that the famous "ankake spa" that I thought was "Japanese" was actually a Nagoya specialty.

I had my first taste of ankake spaghetti back when I was a student, in a manga coffee shop near Nanzan University. My first reaction was "what is this?" That gooey brown sauce and that spicy taste; it was different from any spaghetti I had ever had before. But, for some reason, I just couldn't get enough of it.

Now, I live in Meito ward and on my way to the station there is a small ankake spaghetti restaurant. I'd walked or cycled by it every day

but I'd never gone in. One evening, I was returning from a business trip outside the city and I knew I would be coming home late. I called my wife: "Honey, I think it's best if I grab a bite somewhere on the way home so it's less trouble for you", to which she replied "why don't you do that". That was the answer I was hoping for. I entered that little ankake shop.

I didn't know what to order so I asked for a "regular" ankake spaghetti and a few minutes later, I was served a large plate of pasta covered in brown sauce. I took a bite, "that's it, that's the taste"; it was all coming back to me 25 years later! I left the restaurant with a big smile on my face and I've retuned to that little shop many times since then. Ankake spaghetti has become my "reward" at the end of the day when I come home late from business trips. In order to help keep this delicious Nagoya tradition alive, I've written about it in this book and yet again fulfil my duty as food ambassador!

By the way...

Kids' favorite food in Japan

According to research by Gurunavi Inc, the food Japanese kids like the most is curry rice. Curry is originally from India but the Japanese variant is milder and thicker.

10 most popular foods with Japanese kids (2018)

1.Curry rice 2.Sushi 3.Karaage(Fried chicken)
4.Hamburger steak 5.French fries 6.Ramen 7.Yakiniku
8.Omurice(rice covered with an omelet and ketchup) 9.Pizza
10.Fried rice

14 カナダ領事、銭湯へ行く

5人家族のわが家では、誰かの誕生日の夜はきまって外食をします。末娘のももちゃんが10歳をむかえた日、彼女のリクエストは銭湯でした。近くのスーパー銭湯はレストランも併設しているので、家族はなぜか私が出張するときなどによく行っているようです。銭湯なんてひさしぶり！？　少し緊張する私。ここ日本では、たいていのことは妻のあとをついていけば安心。しかし男湯では、息子だけがたよりです。たのむよ、太朗！

妻が必要なもの一式をバッグにつめてくれたので、それを持っていざ出陣。まずはロッカー選び。そして最大の挑戦…スッポンポン。カナダでもジムの更衣室なんかで全裸はめずらしくないのですが、銭湯で

名古屋市内の
スーパー銭湯で
妻とももちゃんと

At sento
with Noriko
and Momoko

背の高い外国人はどうしても目立ってしまいます。私は誰も気にしないから大丈夫！と自分に言い聞かせて、服をぬいでいると、息子はすでに全裸。はずかしいそぶりは、まったくないようです。私はやはり、少し「プライバシー」を保つためにタオルで前をかくしました。すかさず「誰もそんなことしないよ」と息子。

まわりを見回すと、息子の言うとおり、ほとんどの人は堂々と全裸で歩いてます。でもほかにも仲間がいないかさがしていると、それとなくタオルを前においている人も。私がキョロキョロしていると息子はすでにいません。あとを追って勇気をふりしぼり、浴場へ。

いきなり湯船に入ってはいけない…もちろん知っていますよ。小さなイスにすわって、すぐに出なくなってしまうシャワーのボタンを何度も押して、体を洗います。ようやくおフロへ。せっかくティーンエイジャーの息子と裸のつきあいをしようと思っていたのに、肝心の息子は一体どこへ行ってしまったのだろう。湯気がたちこめる中、メガネをかけてない私が息子をさがしだすのは簡単ではありません。私はアチコチいったりきたり。ヘンな外国人がウロウロしていると思われたでしょうね。結局、息子をみつけることはできませんでした。見知らぬオジサンたちと肩をならべ、10分間の入浴を終え、一番早く待ちあわせ場所に到着。食事中、妻に「どうだった？」と聞かれ、「まあね…」と答える私でした。

ラサール領事のおまけ話

銭湯を愛する子どもたち

カナダにも温泉はありますが（ブリティッシュ・コロンビア州に集中しています）、「公衆浴場」と呼べるものはなく、日本でその存在を知ってびっくりしました。日本の「銭湯」ははるか昔の時代の雰囲気で、タイムスリップしたような気分になります。私も銭湯が嫌いではないのだけれど、銭湯「大好き!!」な子どもたちを見ると、日本人の血が流れているのだな～と感じます。

14 The Canadian Consul goes to a public bath (sento)

In our family of 5, it's become a tradition for the family to eat out on the evening of one of our birthdays. On the day of her 10th birthday, our little one, Momoko, requested that we go out to a "sento", a Japanese public bath. There's a super sento not far from our place that has a restaurant and it seems that my wife and kids like to go there when I'm away on business trips. It's been a while since I last went to a sento, so the thought is making me a bit nervous... In Japan, whenever we go to new places or try new things, I just follow my wife and everything works out fine. But in the men's section of the sento, I only have my son as guide! I'm counting on you, Taro!

My wife puts everything we need in small individual bags and we're all set to go! First we have to choose a locker. Then the big challenge, changing into my "birthday suit". Back in Canada, it's normal to get undressed and walk around naked in the changing rooms of gyms or swimming pools but as a tall foreigner in a Japanese sento, I attract a lot of attention. "O.K. no one is looking at me, no one cares" I tell myself as I start to undress. My son is already standing there naked. He is clearly not fazed by any of this. Me, I dangle a small towel in front of me to keep some privacy. My son notices and quips: "no one does that, Dad!"

I looked around. My son is right; most Japanese are walking around naked and clearly worry-free. But I did find some "like-minded" bathers in the lot and a few of them are dangling a towel in front of them - just like me. As I was busy looking for "friends", I noticed my son was no longer with me. I summoned up all my courage and headed for the bathes, alone.

Of course, I know that you shouldn't enter the bathes right away. I sit on one of the little plastic benches in front of a shower and press the handle repeatedly (the water quickly stops unless you press it again and again) as I wash myself. And finally, on to the bathes! I was looking forward to some quality father-son time and what better setting for that than a public bath? But where is my son anyways? The room is full of steam and I don't have my glasses on so finding him is not an easy task. I go back and forth around the bathes looking for him. The Japanese bathers must have been wondering what that big foreigner was doing. I just couldn't find my son. I ended up joining a group of middle-aged strangers. I stayed in the bath for about 10 minutes, got out and was the first in the family at the meeting spot. Later during dinner, my wife asks "so how was it?" my answer "O.K. I guess..."

By the way...

It's in their Japanese blood!

Although there are hot springs in Canada (most of them in British Columbia) there are no public baths so I was surprised to discover they existed in Japan. Japanese "sento" feel like a tradition from a different era, like going back in time. I enjoy my visits but not as much as my kids who love going to the "sento". It must be in their Japanese blood!

15 領事母、日本のトイレに驚く

77歳の母が2017年10月、モントリオールから遊びにきました。私が90年代に学生生活を送っていたころ、母は雑誌の編集長でいそがしく、日本へ来る機会にめぐまれませんでした。それが、エア・カナダ・ルージュの名古屋↔バンクーバー直行便の就航により、ついに長年の夢をかなえたのです。

つえを片手に歩く母をもう少し早く日本に来させてあげたかったのですが、学生時代の小さなアパートでは、母に窮屈(きゅうくつ)な思いをさせたでしょう。

私の現在の住まいはカナダ人による2×4建築で、つくりもカナダスタイルになっていますが、日本的なところもそなえています。母に最初のカルチャーショックを与えた“トイレ”は、冬でも便座があたたかく、おしりを清潔に洗ってくれるおなじみの温水便座です。しかしカナダではまだまれで、母は使ったことがありませんでした。

好奇心旺盛な77歳。ただ問題は、多数のボタンと、ひらがな・漢字の表記です。絵文字はわかりやすいのですが、トイレを使うたびに、何度もボタンを押してはそれが何を意味するのか確認しなければなりませんでした。水びたしになって、ふきとるのが大変だったと大笑いする母。対応策として「前」、「後ろ」、「あたたかい」など紙に書いてはりつけることにしました。

母は熱田神宮への
お参りも楽しみました

Mom enjoyed her
visit at Atsuta Shrine

それからは、母のトイレへの小旅行はいつも快適なものになりました。母はカナダでも日本と同じようなトイレなら高齢者に最高！と話していました。日本では高齢化の進む中で、人々の生活をより快適にするために、つまりハッピーエイジングのために、多くの新製品の開発に力がそそがれていると感じます。日本の企業は海外で新たな顧客開拓の機会を得るかもしれませんね。もしカナダで買うことができれば、母はそれにすぐさまとびつくでしょう。

母の日本旅行の感動は、もちろんトイレだけではありません。母にとっては、名古屋は一番人気のない街でなんかではありませんでしたよ。

ラサール領事のおまけ話

和式トイレの災難

90年代半ばに日本に来たころは、まだ和式便所が多く、家庭でも古い家屋では和式の便器が使われていました。私は和式のトイレが苦手で避けていました。2016年に日本に戻ってくると、和式はほとんどなくなっていて、ホッとしたものです。

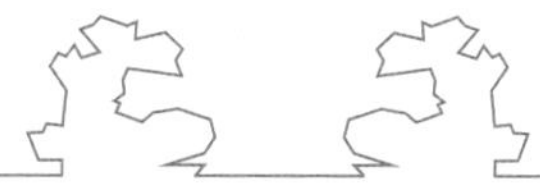

15 The Consul's mother discovers "washlets"

In October 2017, my 77-year-old mother who lives in Montreal travelled all the way to Japan for a visit. When I was a student in Japan back in the 90s, my mother was the busy editor of a magazine in Montreal and she never could find the time to visit her son. Thanks to the new direct flights to Nagoya on Air Canada Rouge, Mom could finally fulfill her longtime dream of visiting Japan.

Mom now walks with the support of a cane so it would have been nice to have her come to Japan when she was younger but then again, back in the 90s, I was living in tiny student's apartment, which was not ideal for hosting.

These days I live in a nice Canadian 2x4 home in Nagoya. The house was built in the Canadian style but it has a few Japanese touches here and there. Mom's first culture shock was on one of the toilet seats in our house, you know the type that cleans the behind and keeps it warm in winter. Those seats are still rare in Canada and Mom had never used one.

Mom's 77-year-old curiosity was piqued, but the problem was that there were so many buttons and their function was written in hiragana and kanji. There were a few easy-to-understand pictograms but for the rest, mom had to push the buttons every time to find out what they did. Mom laughed when she recalled having to clean up the floor

after a squirt from the bidet ended up on the floor. Our solution to the problem? We wrote 'front', 'back' 'warm' on post-it notes that we stuck to the buttons.

Mom's short trips to the toilet were uneventful after that. Mom thought that these "washlets", would be very popular among seniors in Canada. With the greying of society, many Japanese companies have been busy developing new products that promise to make the life of the country's senior citizens easier, the so called "happy aging" phenomenon. For some of these Japanese companies, foreign countries could well become high potential markets to develop. If they were available in Canada, Mom would definitely buy one of those "washlet" toilet seat covers.

Of course, toilet seats were not the highlight of mom's trip to Japan. Mom loved her stay in Nagoya and she definitely doesn't think that it's Japan's "least popular city"!

By the way...

The Japanese toilet landscape has changed...

When I first came to Japan in the mid 90s, there were still many old style "squatting" type public toilets. You could even find them in some older homes. I didn't like them and avoided them like the plague! When I came back to Japan in 2016, I was very happy to discover that most of them had disappeared!

16 領事娘、おいらんになる

３週間の母の滞在で、一番の心に残る思い出は、京都への小旅行でもなく、大須でした。というのは孫娘さくらの晴れ姿をそこで見ることができたからです。

大須での大道町人祭の中のおいらん道中に、長女さくらが参加することになったのです。当時高校生だった長女は、人生の大半を海外ですごし、週末の日本語学校は国語と数学が中心で、日本の歴史についてはほとんど学んでいません。広告でおいらん募集の記事をみて、昔のお姫さまみたいになりたい！くらいのノリで応募したのでした。

ちなみに、３人の子どものうち、さくらのかわいらしさは（自慢をおゆるしください）ママから来ているってパパは認めざるをえません（なんてね！）。さくらは面接によばれ、おいらんのひとりに選ばれたのです。

いよいよ当日。１時間も前から、大須の商店街にはすでに人だかりができていました。よく見ると、カメラをかかえた男性陣が場所とりをしています。海外でこういった光景を目にしたことはありませんが、カメラを趣味にする日本人が多いですね。みなさん、プロなみの高価な機材を持っています。ちなみにわが家は、ほとんど写真を撮らないので、この日も義父から借りたデジカメを持参。

「大須太夫（だゆう）のおな～り～」。３人の女の子が伝統的なかつらと化粧

をし、20kg もある衣装と15cm の高げたで、八文字を踏みながら登場。その 3 人の真ん中に娘のさくらが黒の着物を着ていかにも太夫然とし、堂々と立っているではありませんか。私たちは興奮の絶頂でした。舞台でお披露目後、大須の商店街をねり歩きます。私たちも娘を追いかけます。しばらくして、ここ数年は外出にはつえを必要とする母を見失い、迷子になったかと心配していると、なんと行列の最前列にいるではありませんか。急に若返ってしまったようで、母は、つえを忘れて小走りしているのです。それを見た私は、大須の小さな奇跡だ！と思ったのでした。

さくらの
おいらん姿の写真。
かつら、着物、化粧と
どれもきれい！

Sakura as an Oiran.
The wig, dress and makeup
are all beautiful

ラサール領事のおまけ話

おいらんは知られていないけれど…

「おいらん」という言葉を知っているカナダ人はめったにいませんが、「サムライ」はよく知られています。日本の剣士はとても「クール」なイメージで、特に男の子たちには大人気。「ニンジャ」も同様に人気があります。欧米の「サムライ」「ニンジャ」人気は、50 年代や60 年代の黒澤映画によるところが大きいでしょう。

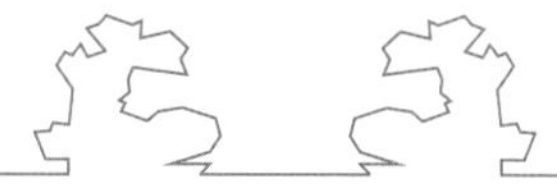

16 The Consul's daughter becomes an "Oiran" courtesan

The highlight of Mom's 3-week stay in Japan wasn't her short trip to Kyoto, it was the time she spent in Nagoya's Osu district. That's where she got to see her granddaughter Sakura all dressed up in the most beautiful traditional Japanese clothing.

Our eldest daughter, Sakura, joined the Oiran procession during the Osu Street Performers' Festival. Sakura was then a high school student in Nagoya but she had spent most of her young life abroad. While we lived abroad, she attended a special Japanese school on weekends. The curriculum focused mostly on the Japanese language and on math but left little time for Japanese history. Sakura saw a notice in the paper for oiran auditions and loved the idea of becoming a "Japanese princess" from the past. And on a whim, she sent in an application.

By the way - and allow me to brag a little - I have to admit that our daughter Sakura's beauty definitely comes from her mother! The organizers called Sakura in for an interview and she was chosen as one of the oirans for this year's procession.

And the big day arrived! One hour before the event, a crowd had already gathered in the Osu market. I noticed that a group of, largely male, photographers had set up their gear in front of the temple.

I don't think I've ever seen a similar site at an event in Canada but photography is a popular hobby in Japan. All the amateur photographers in Osu that night had professional looking equipment. We aren't camera buffs so that day, we borrowed my father-in-law's camera.

"Osu tayu no ona-ri-" The 3 young women wearing traditional wigs, makeup and full garb weighing 20kg, made their way on the Osu stage performing the "figure eight walk" perched on 15cm tall wooden sandals. And there she was, our Sakura, standing in the middle of the 3 girls in a black kimono - and in character - as she made her way regally across the stage. After the presentation of the 3 girls, the procession made its way through the Osu market with the oirans performing their special walk. The whole family followed them. A few minutes into our chase, we noticed that grandma was no longer with us. I worried that we'd lost her but she soon reappeared; there she was, practically at the head of the parade! All the excitement had given her a jolt of youthful energy and she was walking briskly, almost running. Looks like she no longer needed the cane she'd been using on outings these last few years. Seeing her like that, I thought to myself: I just witnessed a small miracle in Osu!

By the way...

What is an Oiran?

The "Oiran" were courtesans in Japan. They were distinguished from other prostitutes for being highly regarded as entertainers. They were educated in traditional artforms and were expected to be well-read in order to converse with wit and elegance with their patrons. The highest rank for Oiran courtesan was "tayu". An Oiran courtesan parade is held in October every year during the Osu Street Performers' Festival.

17 いまでもクールな大須

長女さくらがおいらん道中に参加した大須は、私にとって思い出深い地です。

着任してすぐ、90年代中ごろに出会った友人・サイトウと久々に再会するため、大須にでかけることにしました。

私が名古屋大で修士課程に進んでいた90年代後半、インターネット時代の波がきていました。私もその波にとび乗ったひとり。コンピューターの組みたてをすべて自分でやっていました。そのころの大須は、まさに名古屋の秋葉原で、コンピューターショップが軒をならべ、私は毎週のように足を運んだものです。新しいゲームや部品を見つけると目をかがやかせ、けっこうな額をつぎこんでいました。

大須に近づいてくると、車からでも街の変化に気づきました。かつて

大須はイベントも
サンバにラテンアメリカ
フェスティバルなど
国際色豊か

Brazilian samba
held in Osu

のコンピューターショップのほとんどがなくなっていたのです。90年代には、大須のような特別な商店街に出向いてしか手に入らない製品が多くありました。それがいまはネット販売に一変したのです。どこからでも、すぐになんでもさがせて、しかも安い。皮肉にも、大須が育ててくれた私のようなコンピューターオタクが、オンラインショッピングの便利さに最初にとびつく消費者になったのでした。中部のオタクの聖地であった大須は、その信者たちがネットへくらがえしたことで、終わりをつげることになったのです。

そして、私が日本を離れていたこの20年の間に、いまどきの若者むけの洋服店やおしゃれなカフェやレストランが増え、大須をヒップな色にぬりかえています。

変化はいつも悪いとはかぎりません。若者に人気の原宿や、外国人がよく集まる六本木、電化製品でにぎわう秋葉原のような要素が、コンパクトに大須という商店街にまとまっています。ムダなくまわれる便利さがあります。この便利さこそがインターネット世代には重要なキーワードではないでしょうか？ 20年たっても大須はまだ、私にとって名古屋でもっともクールな場所なのです。

ラサール領事のおまけ話

大須のおもちゃ屋さん

90年代の大須には、“町のおっちゃんおばちゃん”がやっている、個人商店がまだたくさんありました。チープなプラスチックの玩具を売る古いおもちゃ屋さんを、今でも鮮やかに思い出せます。小さかった娘に世界の国々を覚えさせようと、世界地図のパズルをその類のお店で買ったこともよく覚えています。

17 Osu, still the coolest place in Nagoya

The Osu district where our eldest daughter Sakura joined the Oiran Procession is a place full of memories for me.

Not long after I became consul in Nagoya, I met up with my good friend Saito whom I've known since the mid 90s and for our reunion we decided to go to Osu.

I was pursuing a master's degree at Nagoya University in the late 90s just when the internet was starting and I dove head first in that first wave. I even used to put together my own computers. Back then, Osu was really Nagoya's Akihabara and you could find row after row of computer shops on its streets. I would go down there almost every week. I remember the pleasure I'd get from finding the latest computer games or the latest parts and accessories for my computer. I spent a lot of money in Osu.

As we were approaching Osu by car, I could already see how the district had changed. Gone were most of the computer stores of my student days. Back in the 90s, there were still many products you could only find in specific shopping districts like Osu. But the advent of online shopping changed all that. Now you can pretty much buy anything from anywhere around the world, and it's cheap! It's a bit ironic that the computer geeks that Osu helped raise were among the earliest adopters of online shopping. Osu, once holy ground for

the computer geeks that flocked there would lose its faithful to the internet; an era was ending…

During my 20-year absence, clothing stores and restaurants targeting a young urban clientele had replaced many of the computer shops, giving the whole area a much “hipper” vibe.

Change is not always a bad thing. Osu now has a bit of the youth of Harajuku; it's also a place where foreigners (like me) gather to have a good time like Roppongi; it even has a few computers stores left as well, like Akihabara. It's all on a much smaller scale but, heh, it's all in one convenient location, and convenience is important in the internet age, right? 20 years later, to me, Osu is still the coolest place in Nagoya.

Latin America Festival in Osu

By the way…

Mom-and-pop shops

Back in the 90s there were still many mom-and-pop stores in Osu. I vividly remember seeing old toy stores that sold cheap plastic toys. I remember stopping in one of them and buying a puzzle map of the world for my young daughter, to help her learn and memorize the world's many countries.

ラサール領事のインタビュー！

名古屋の魅力を掘り下げようと、独自で名古屋の商店街や企業幹部を取材して歩いているラサール領事。大好きな大須の商店街連盟会長・堀田聖司さんに、大須の魅力をうかがいました。

大須の成長戦略は『オープンな心』

私がはじめて大須を訪れたのは1994年。当時は南山大学の留学生でした。「現代」を象徴するコンピューターショップに、昭和のレトロな雰囲気ただよう商店街、由緒ある大須観音。時代の新旧が融合した場所でした。コンピューターオタクだった私は、毎週末大須へかよい、新しいソフトウェアや部品を物色していました。

2016年、12年ぶりに来日し、最初に訪ねたのはやっぱり大須。以前とかわらず活気があり、楽しい場所でしたが、留学生時代のコンピューターショップは消え、ファッショナブルでエキゾチックな洋服屋と世界各国のレストランがたちならんでいました。「外国人とのつきあいがウマい！」と感動しました。

そこ大須商店街連盟の堀田会長に連絡。いちファンとして、大須商店街再開発の秘密をたずねてみたのです。

―大須は外国人に非常にオープンです。外国人経営者を積極的に誘致しているのですか？

いいえ、特には。大須には約1200の店舗がありますが、毎年その50～80店舗は入れかわっています。オーナーさんへの偏見や先入観は持ちません。日本人、外国人問わずです。たとえば、全身タトゥーでおおわれたオーナーは、栄や名駅エリアでは敬遠されるでしょうが、大

大須商店街連盟会長の堀田聖司さんと

With Mr. Shoji Hotta
(Head of the Osu Merchants' Association)

須ではまともなビジネスプランや責任感のある方なら、どなたでも歓迎します。

―大須では宣伝費をかけないときいていますが、本当ですか？

いいえ、かならずしもそうではありません。チラシなどに使う宣伝費は比較的少ないですが、祭りやユニークなイベントの開催が、大須の広報活動になっています。

たとえば、新元号「令和」発表の際、地元の方々むけに楽しいライブイベントを企画しました。そこにメディアの方を呼ぶことで、ちょっとした宣伝効果をねらっていました。

人脈をいかして、地元の学校などを招き、ドキドキしながら迎えた当日。うれしいことに（ちょうど休み中だったのはラッキー）期待以上の人が集まり、にぎやかな風景が報道されました。その結果、地域メディアだけでなく、全国ニュースで大須がとりあげられる形となりました。

なるほど！「戦略」は特になかったものの、長年の「寛容な姿勢」が大須を繁栄させたことにまちがいありません。「変化」だけでなく「違い」への寛容性。20年前と変わらず、大須は私にとって名古屋のもっともクールな場所でした。

The Canadian Consul interviews Mr.Shoji Hotta, head of the Osu Merchants' Association

Osu's growth strategy: an open heart

The first time I came to Osu was in 1994, when I was a student at Nanzan University. The very modern computer shops, the "somewhat old" Showa era shopping arcade, and the "very old" temples like Osu Kannon made for a fascinating and eclectic mix. Later, as a graduate student at Nagoya University, I lived through a very intense computer "otaku" phase and went on an almost weekly pilgrimage to Osu looking for new software or parts to feed my addiction. I came back to Japan in 2016 after a 12-year absence and one of the first places I visited after my return was Osu. And just as I suspected, it was still as vibrant and fun as before. Gone were the computer shops, many replaced by fashionable clothing stores and Vietnamese, Turkish and Brazilian restaurants – just to name a few of the many cuisines people can sample there. I was impressed by how well Osu was welcoming of foreigners.

As a great fan of Osu, I thought I'd reach out to the Osu Merchants Associations to learn about the area's secret for reinventing itself.

Osu is very welcoming of foreigners. Do you actively target foreigners in your business plan?

Not really but there are about 1200 shops in Osu of which about

50 to 80 change hands any given year. As a community, we've always welcomed various types of shop owners and clients without prejudice. It's not only foreigners who benefit from this open attitude, Japanese do as well. For example, a tattoo covered shop owner might have a hard time being taken seriously as a businessman in the Sakae or Nagoya station area, but as long as his business plan makes sense and he's a responsible owner, he's welcome in Osu.

I read somewhere that you didn't spend any money on advertising, is that true?

Not exactly. We do spend some money on leaflets and such but relatively little. On the other hand, we try to generate exposure in creative ways. For example, we created a live event around the official announcement of the naming of the new Reiwa era and we invited journalist to cover it. We used our networks in the local community to spread the word and raise a good crowd. We crossed our fingers and hoped for the best – we didn't want to press to show up only to see just a few individuals! To our relief, the turnout was very good and it made for great TV! Osu ended up getting lots of local and even national coverage.

Interesting…! It turns out that Osu doesn't have an active strategy to attract foreigners . But if they don't have a "strategy", they certainly have an "attitude" of openness that has served them very well over the years. First, an openness to change but also an openness to difference. Just like it was 20 years ago, Osu to me is still the coolest part of Nagoya.

18 領事息子の夏休み

長い夏休みがはじまる前、日本人の妻は息子に２つの選択肢を与えました。去年お世話になった近所のファミリーレストランのアルバイトに２カ月間行くか、それとも２週間の座禅修行をするか。

私たち夫婦は、オンラインゲームばかりしている息子を心配しています。将来どこで生活したいのか聞くと、「インターネットと米があればどこでもいい」との答え。10年以上前に、私が勝手に買ってしまった家

座禅修行をする息子
Taro in zazen meditation

庭用ゲーム機が「諸悪の根源」だったと、妻はいまでも私をチクチク責めるのです。息子のゲーム好きが私ゆずりなのは認めますが、17歳の息子はそろそろ将来を意識しなくてはならない年ごろにきています。

まよった末の息子の決断は、京都のお寺行きでした。サウナのようなキッチンで、ひたすら油でギトギトの鉄板を洗う、息子いわく「軍隊のようなアルバイト」を選ばないのは想定内でした。お寺では禅の生活を通じて、インターネットがつながらない環境で、人生は「刹那的な遊び」だけじゃないことを学び、彼の日本側のルーツを体感し、精進料理で軽いダイエット。完全なる「ゲームデトックスセラピー」です。

いざ新幹線に乗って、ひとり京都へ。すぐ翌日、座禅の合間に息子から「明日下山する」との電話。「暑い、足がいたい、頭がいたい…」。エアコンもなく快適とはほど遠い環境で、「選択」がまちがいだったと思ったようです。妻は息子をはげましつつ「いま帰ったら携帯は解約ね」と、ちょっとした脅しも。私にも使う「アメとムチ作戦」です。

3日目になると、あれほど文句ばかり言っていた息子からの電話がパタリとなくなりました。作業で草刈りをした際、アレルギーで湿疹がでたことを幸いに座禅修行は10日間に短縮され、予定より早く下山しました。帰宅後、第一声は「肉が食べたい」でした。効果があったのかまだわかりませんが、応援してるよ！　ガンバレ、息子！

ラサール領事のおまけ話

モントリオールはゲームの街！

私の故郷・モントリオールは、東京、ロンドン、サンフランシスコ、テキサス州オースティンに次いで、世界で5番目にゲーム開発が盛んな都市。モントリオールには140ものゲーム制作会社があるのです。太朗もゲームをプレイするほうにではなく、作るほうにエネルギーをそそいでくれたらいいのですけれど…。

18 My son's summer vacation

Before the start of the summer vacations, my wife gave our son two choices: he could either go back and work for 2 months at the same neighborhood restaurant as last year, or he could go to a Buddhist temple for 2 weeks of "ascetic" zazen meditation...

Our son spends many hours every day playing online video games and this (bad) habit of his has got his mother and I worried. Recently, when we asked him where he'd like to live in the future, his answer was: "anywhere is fine as long as I've got rice and internet access". To this day, my wife keeps reminding me of the TV gaming console I bought (without her permission) over 10 years ago; "That's when it all started," she complains. I have to admit our son gets his love of video games from me but at any rate, he's now 17 years old and it's time for him to think about his future.

After thinking it through, our son chose the Kyoto temple meditation "plan"... as expected. We kinda knew that he would not find the idea of spending another summer cleaning oily frypans in a hot and sweaty kitchen (our son referred to last year's experience as "like being in the army") very appealing. At the Buddhist temple, our son would put a bit of "Zen" in his life and learn that life is not just about "fleeting pleasure" all the while connecting with his Japanese roots. Throw in the "shojin cuisine" (vegetarian Buddhist style) that could

help him shed a few pounds and you've got the makings of a perfect "video game detox therapy".

Our son got on the train and off he went to Kyoto. The very next day between two sessions of "zazen", we get a call from him. "I'm leaving this place tomorrow" he declared, "it's hot, my feet hurt and my head hurts…" Far removed from the comforts of home with no air conditioning, our son was having second thoughts about the "plan" he had chosen. I could hear my wife offering him some words of encouragement on the phone; she also threw in a few light threats: "if you come back now, we'll cut your smart phone account". My wife uses the same "carrot and stick approach" with me.

After the third day, our son, who was so bitter at first, suddenly went quiet. No more phone calls. Later, while he was doing some weeding choirs in the temple garden, our son had an allergic reaction and developed a rash on his skin. That was the perfect excuse for him to come home early, only 10 days into his stay. His first words after arriving home: "I want to eat meat!" Did this stay at the temple help with the video gaming addiction? Well, the jury is still out on that one but either way, we're rooting for you! "Gambare Taro!"

By the way...

What is Zen?

There are several Buddhist sects in Japan, and there are 3 main Zen sects: Soto, Rinzai and Obaku. The aim of Zen is to meditate in order to eliminate hesitations or delusions and awaken to the truth. One of the practices used to acquire serenity of mind is "zazen", which means to sit in silent meditation. Shojin cuisine, which bans eating meat and replaces it with tofu or seaweed, is also part of Zen.

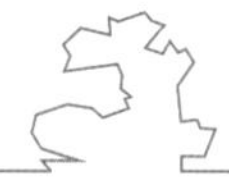

ラサール領事のなごや日記

19 カナダ人はプライベートを大切にする

2016年に日本に赴任したころ、過労自殺がしきりにニュースで流れていました。私が名古屋大に留学していた90年代後半と、日本の労働環境はあまり変わっていないように思いました。

私が学生だったころからの20年来の友・カズは、産婦人科医師。超多忙な勤務を送りながらも、私がフランス語を教えたことが縁で親しくなりました。彼の小学生だった息子たちもいまでは30代。2人とも愛知県内の企業で、ソフトウェアエンジニアとして働いています。

ひとりは、職場近くでひとり暮らしをしています。残業が多いため、通勤時間の節約が理由とはトホホ…。でも、もうひとりは午後7時ごろには帰宅でき、有給休暇もしっかりととれるそうで、私の予想をいい意味で裏切る状況でした。

もちろん、カナダでも残業はあります。でも圧倒的なちがいは、プライベートな時間をとることが社会的に尊重されているところです。16年の伊勢志摩サミットの前日、カナダのトルドー首相は公務を休み、夫人と結婚記念日を祝いました。ワークライフバランスの実例をトップ自らが示しています。カナダでは夕食を家族で食べることはごく普通。そして多くの人が、まだ残っている一日をどうすごすか、躍起になるのです。

私の場合はボードゲーム制作に没頭しています。子どもたちには、「好きなことをさがす努力をしなさい」としつこいほど言っています。

憧れの東京で
大学生活スタート。
頑張れさくら！

Sakura started university
life in Tokyo.
Gambare Sakura !

好きなことであれば、たとえ長時間であっても、つらくても続けることができます。

私の長女は、悩んだ結果、東京の大学に進むことを決めました。10年後、娘が社会人になっているころ、日本がいまよりさらに働きやすい環境で、生活に比重をおける社会になっていることを期待しています。

ラサール領事のおまけ話

カナダの残業を“させにくい”制度

カナダでは一般的に、残業をすればもちろん残業代がつきますが、まず残業すること自体への承認を上司からもらわなければいけません。残業が認められず、帰宅して仕事は翌日以降にまわすよううながされることもよくあるでしょう。残業代は一般的に、通常の時間帯の1.5倍支払うことになっていますから…。

19 Canadians value their private time

Just when I started working as consul back in 2016, a new case of "karoshi" (death by overwork) was all over the news in Japan. I worried that the Japanese workplace hadn't changed much since the 90s when I first lived here as a student.

My good friend Kazu is an obstetrician and we've been friends since my student days in Japan, over 20 years ago. Kazu is a very busy man but he would find time to pursue hobbies like studying French and I was his teacher for a few years, which is how we became friends. His two sons, who were in elementary school when we first met, were now in their early thirties. Both were working in Aichi as software engineers.

One of his boys is living alone in an apartment near his office. He chose that location because he was working overtime so often that he wanted to get home quickly after work. Not good... But I was pleasantly surprised to find out that his other son had found a much better working environment where he gets to leave the office around 7:00PM and he can freely take all his holidays.

Of course, some people do work overtime in Canada as well. But the big difference between both countries is that Canadian society values and respects a person's "private time". In 2016, the day before the Ise Summit in Japan, Canadian Prime Minister Trudeau took time

off from his official duties to celebrate his wedding anniversary with his wife. A good example of work-life balance right from the top! In Canada, it's very common for families to have dinner together every night. For many Canadians, it becomes a (pleasant) "problem" to find ways to use that free time at the end of the day.

I've used that extra free time myself to dab into creative pursuits like making board games. "Try to find something you really like", I keep telling my kids – so often that they're tired of hearing me say it. But the reason is simple: if they can find something they love, they'll be able to do it for very long hours even if it's very demanding.

It was one of those hard to make "life decisions" but our eldest daughter decided to attend a university in Tokyo (rather than in Canada). 10 years from now, when our daughter has started her career, I hope that the Japanese workplace has continued to improve and that Japanese society has learned to place even greater value on its workers' quality of life.

By the way...

Work style reform in Japan

In 2019, 2,018 people committed suicide for work-related problems in Japan. The government is aiming to reduce the number of people working more than 60 hours a week to 5% of the workforce by 2020. The target will be hard to reach since 6.9% of the workforce (3.97 million people!) fall into that category today. Although overwork remains a problem, the public's interest in the issue has been growing lately and the Japanese Parliament enacted a work style reform law in 2018.

20 フランス語の可能性

カナダは航空宇宙産業にも力をいれていることをご存じでしょうか。ボンバルディア社はボーイング、エアバスにつづく世界3位の民間航空機メーカーに育ちました。

ここ中部地域でも、航空宇宙産業が注目されています。機体組み立てを請け負う愛知の東明工業（とうめいこうぎょう）は、2017年カナダに法人を設立されました。先日、その社員の方に「フランス語を勉強できるところを知っていますか？」ときかれ、名古屋の本山にある、アリアンス・フランセーズという、フランス政府公認助成の語学学校をすすめました。英語とフランス語を公用語にもつカナダで、ボンバルディア本社のあるケベック州モントリオールは、もっとも大きなフランス語圏なのです。

私もケベック州出身です。祖先は1700年ごろにフランスから北米に

幼いころの私（左）と
双子の弟

That's me (left) with my fraternal twin brother in the summer of 1973 when we were 5 yrs old and enjoyed watching Leo

移住しました。カナダ全人口の1/4ぐらいを占めるフランス系の約8割がケベック州に住んでいます。家での会話はフランス語。幼いころ、よく見ていた日本アニメのテレビ番組はフランス語の吹きかえ版でした。いまでもジャングル大帝レオのテーマソングはフランス語で歌えます。

話がそれましたが、カナダは欧州連合（EU）と自由貿易協定（FTA）を結んでいます。2017年は日本がEUと経済連携協定（EPA）を妥結。さらには2018年1月、日本とカナダは包括的先進的環太平洋連携協定（CPTPP）の合意にいたりました。これにより航空宇宙産業も、北米や欧州の会社とのビジネスチャンスが期待できます。中部地域のフランス語のニーズ拡大にもつながるでしょう。私の母国語を多くの人が学ぼうとしてくれるのは、うれしいことです。もし私を見かけたら、気軽に「Bonjour！」と声をかけてください。フランス語版レオの歌を披露しますよ。

ラサール領事のおまけ話

フランス語を公用語とする国

フランス語は29カ国で公用語として使われています。人口の多い順に並べると
1. コンゴ民主共和国　2. フランス　3. カナダ　4. マダガスカル　5. カメルーン　6. コートジボワール　7. ニジェール　8. ブルキナファソ　9. マリ　10. セネガル　11. チャド　12. ギニア　13. ルワンダ　14. ベルギー　15. ベナン　16. ブルンジ　17. ハイチ　18. スイス　19. トーゴ　20. コンゴ共和国　21. 中央アフリカ　22. ガボン　23. 赤道ギニア　24. ジブチ　25. コモロ　26. ルクセンブルグ　27. バヌアツ　28. セイシェル　29. モナコ　となります。

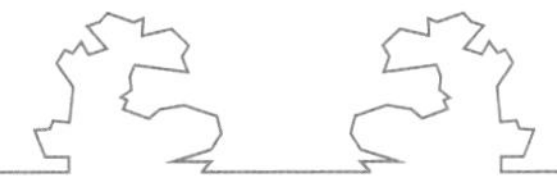

20 French opens doors

You might be aware that the aerospace industry is a top priority for Canada and our very own Bombardier is the world's third largest civil aircraft manufacturer after Boeing and Airbus.

The aerospace industry has been getting a lot of attention in the Chubu region as well. In 2017, Aichi based aircraft parts supplier Tohmei Kogyo incorporated in Canada and the other day, one of their employees came up to me and asked, "do you know where I can take French lessons?" I recommended the Alliance Française, a school that is run and partially funded by the French government. Both French and English are official languages in Canada and Bombardier's headquarters are located in Montreal, in the Province of Quebec, the biggest French speaking area in Canada.

I'm from Quebec myself and my ancestors left France to settle in North America around 1700. About one quarter of the Canadian population is of French origin and about 80 percent of them live in the province of Quebec. I spoke French at home. The Japanese animation I watched on TV as a child was all dubbed in French. Even today, I can still sing the theme song of "Jungle Taitei Leo"... in French!

I digress... Canada has entered a free trade accord with the European Union. In 2017, Japan and the European Union agreed to an economic partnership of their own. Moreover, in January of 2018,

Japan and Canada concluded the Comprehensive and Progressive Agreement for Trans Pacific Partnership (CPTPP) agreement – often referred to as TPP11 in Japan. These agreements should mean opportunities for the Japanese aerospace industry in both the European and North American markets. It could also mean increased demand for the French language in the Chubu area. The thought of more people wanting to learn my mother tongue makes me very happy. If you ever see me some day, don't be shy and say "bonjour!" I just might perform the "Leo" theme song for you, in French!

By the way...

French speaking countries

French is the official language in 29 countries around the world. Here they are in order of population:

1.Democratic Republic of the Congo 2.France 3.Canada 4.Madagascar 5.Cameroon 6.Ivory Coast 7.Niger 8.Burkina Faso 9.Mali 10.Sénégal 11.Chad 12.Guinea 13.Rwanda 14.Belgium 15.Benin 16.Burundi 17.Haiti 18.Switzerland 19.Togo 20.Republic of Congo 21.Central African Republic 22.Gabon 23.Equatorial Guinea 24.Djibouti 25.Comoros 26.Luxembourg 27.Vanuatu 28.Seychelles 29.Monaco

21 弁護士から外交官に転身、フツウです

ある日、愛知県弁護士会から来訪がありました。名古屋に住むカナダ人たちの法的なニーズはなにか、などの意見交換がおもな目的でした。彼らもビジネスチャンスをさがしているわけで、私自身も弁護士のはしくれとしてちょっと興味があったのです。

1992年に私は弁護士となりました。しかし、1年もたたないうちに大学に戻り、94年に日本へ留学する機会にめぐまれたのでした。日本の人は、私が「弁護士」であることを知ると、みんなきまっておどろきました。あとでわかったのは、日本では弁護士が非常に少なく、せっかく資格をとっても私のようにちがう道を進む人は、変わり者らしいです。

90年代半ば、新弁護士の登録者数は日本では年に800人。カナダでは、人口は日本の1/4ですが、年間約3,000人。ただ、ほぼ半数が転職します。

2016年の夏に再来日してすぐに、日本の法的状況の変化を、私は地下鉄の車内で気づきました。私が留学生のころは、弁護士の広告はなかったはずです。現在では、新弁護士の登録者数は年に1,500人まで増加しているとのこと。全体としては、30,000人にものぼるそうです。行政書士も増加しているので、私が「仕事は十分にありますか？」と少しストレートに質問すると、彼らは苦笑いをしていました。

逆に、「カナダの弁護士は、そんなにかんたんにキャリアを変えて、

なにをするのですか？」とたずねられました。「たとえば外交官ですかね」。ちなみに私の東京の上司も、もと弁護士。カナダの外務省には、弁護士の資格をもっている仲間は少なくありません。ロースクールのクラスメートの中にはモントリオールで広告会社「Sid Lee」をたちあげた者もいます。世界的にも有名になったその会社は、2015年、博報堂に買収され、さらに成長しています（夢は追いつづけなくちゃね！）。

これから日本も、カナダと同じように、いろいろな分野で「モト弁護士」の活躍を期待できる時代になってくるのではないでしょうか。

弁護士バッジは日本特有。
私の弁護士IDはコレ！
今でも会員費を払っている
ので「現役」です

My lawyer association membership card. I pay my membership fee every year so I can honestly say "I'm a lawyer"

ラサール領事のおまけ話

今でも現役です！

私は1992年にケベック弁護士会に入会、以来毎年、年会費を払い続けています。ですから今でも「現役の弁護士」と名乗ることができるわけなのです…が、妻は「何年も弁護士として働いていないんだから、" ペーパー弁護士 " でしょ！」と手厳しいです…。

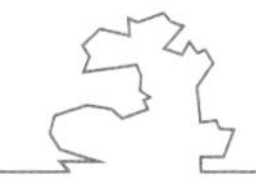

21 Going from lawyer to diplomat – it's normal!

The other day, the Aichi Lawyer's Association dropped by my office for a quick visit. Apparently, they wanted to discuss how best to support the legal needs of Nagoya's Canadian community. These lawyers were essentially looking for business opportunities – we all are – and, being a lawyer myself (at least by training) I was curious to hear what they had to say.

I became a lawyer in 1992, but less than a year later, I left my young career to go back to university and, in 1994, I was lucky enough to get an opportunity to come to Japan to study. People in Japan were always surprised when they heard that I was a "lawyer". I soon found out why: there were so few lawyers in Japan that you would have to be half-crazy to turn your back on a legal career once you'd earned the title.

Back in the mid-90s, the number of new lawyers admitted to the Japanese bar stood at 800. Canada with only a quarter of Japan's population admitted 3,000 new lawyers every year. Although in Canada, half of all lawyers eventually leave the legal profession for a different career.

After my return to Japan in 2016, I got my first hint that Japan's legal environment had changed while riding the Nagoya subway. There were ads for legal services in the cars. That wasn't the case

when I was a student in Japan in the mid-90s. Nowadays, Japan admits over 1,500 new lawyers to the bar every year and the country now counts over 30,000 lawyers. The number of “Gyosei-shoshi” (legal specialists who handle minor administrative procedures) is also growing. I asked my guests, rather bluntly, “is there enough work for all the lawyers?” Their first response was an uneasy smile.

They had questions for me as well, “if it’s so easy to change careers in Canada, what do lawyers do after they leave the profession?”, “well, some become diplomats…” By the way, it’s not just me, my boss in Tokyo is also a lawyer. In fact, there are quite a few diplomats with legal credentials working within the Canadian department of foreign affairs. One of my friends from Law School went on to create “Sid Lee”, a very successful advertising agency that was acquired by Hakuhodo in 2015. And Sid Lee is still growing! (‘Follow your dreams’ goes the saying…)

In the coming years, something tells me that just like in Canada, we’ll see more “ex-lawyers” making their mark in many fields in Japan.

By the way...

Still a bona fide lawyer

I became a member of the Quebec Bar Association in 1992 and I’ve paid my membership dues every year since then. Even today, I can still claim that I am a bona fide “lawyer”. But my wife reminds me that I haven’t really practised law in many years, which makes me what the Japanese call a “paper lawyer”...

22 LGBT支援、日本は懐(ふところ)が広い!?

2018年9月、栄での「虹色どまんなかパレード」に招待されました。このイベントは、地元のLGBT(レズビアン、ゲイ、バイセクシュアル、トランスジェンダー)コミュニティーやその支援者らが、より多くの人々に問題意識を持ってもらえるように企画したものです。カナダのトルドー首相も母国で同様のイベントに参加し、多様性や人権支援に力をそそいでいますので、私もそれにならい、ここ名古屋でサポートできたらと思っています。

カナダのLGBTを支援するイベント“プライド”は、華やかに着かざった人々がパレードに参加して、とても活気があります。名古屋も例外でなく、リオのカーニバルのようにドレスアップした人もいました。

一方で、問題の深刻さにも気づかされました。たとえば、同性愛カップルは住まいをみつけるのがむずかしく、そのような人々に不動産を紹介するサービスや、学校や職場でLGBTの差別をなくし、理解を深める講演を行う団体などが参加していました。

90年代に日本に私が最初にやってきたとき、テレビを見ておどろいたのを覚えています。シャンソン歌手として活躍していた美輪明宏さんや、女性もうらやみそうなかっこいいピーターさん。ウイットにとんだ会話で楽しませてくれるおすぎさんとピーコさん。そんな人々を見て、日本の多様性をうけいれる力をカナダ以上に感じました。

素敵なドレス！
雨の日に光を
もたらしました。私の灰色の
スーツよりもずっと元気に
してくれますね

I love that dress! It brought
a bit of sunshine on a rainy day.
Much livelier than
my grey suit!

20年たってまた名古屋に戻ってきて、マツコ・デラックスさんをはじめ、さらに多様性あふれるタレントがテレビをにぎわせていますね。日本人の懐の深さは健在のようですが、身近な現実の世界は、テレビほどには簡単ではないようにも思えます。

本当にうけいれられていれば、自らがLGBTである事実をかくす必要もないでしょう。だって（いい意味で）誰も気にしないんですから。差別や偏見がなく、多様性をみとめ、平等であるとき、テレビの世界と一般社会との受容力のギャップは消え去るでしょう。

ラサール領事のおまけ話

カナダは同姓婚を認める国

カナダは2005年に、同姓婚を認めた4番目の国になりました。ヨーロッパ以外では初めてです。最初に同姓婚を合法化したのはオランダで、2001年のことでした。

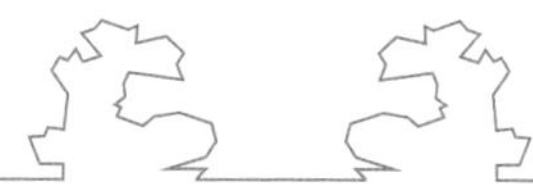

22 In support of LGBT rights in "tolerant" Japan

In September, 2017, the organizers of the Rainbow Parade invited me to join their parade in Sakae. The event is organized by the local LGBT community and their supporters, to raise awareness about the problems they face. Canadian Prime Minister Trudeau has made it a point to join similar events back home in support of diversity and human rights, so I thought I'd follow his example and offer my support in Nagoya.

"Pride" events in Canada are lively affairs and are often attended by some flamboyant personalities. Nagoya was no exception and one of the participants was dressed in full "Rio Carnival" regalia.

While the mood was festive, there was also a more serious side to the event. For example, a real estate agency was offering to help couples find rental properties in Nagoya, which can be a problem for some same sex couples. Another association was offering to hold school and workplace info sessions to improve the acceptance of gays and lesbians.

When I first lived in Japan back in the 90s, I remember being surprised by how ubiquitous the gay community was on Japanese television. There was cross-dressing "chanson" (French style) singer Akihiro Miwa. There was also the strikingly feminine Peter who probably made a few women jealous with his good looks. There

were also others like Peeco and his brother Osugi who entertained with their sharp wit. Overall, my impression of Japan was that the acceptance of homosexuality ran very deep, possibly deeper than in Canada.

20 years later, I've returned to Japan to find that these entertainers have been joined by new ones such as the hugely popular Matsuko Deluxe who livens up our TV screens. Japanese tolerance to diversity appears to be as healthy as ever but when we look around us, I get the impression that the acceptance of gays and lesbians in Japan is possibly not as deep as it appears on TV.

A true measure of tolerance will be when no one has to hide the fact that they are gay – because no one cares! (I mean that in a good way) When there is no discrimination or prejudice, when diversity is valued, the "acceptance gap" between the world of Japanese television and the rest of society will fade away.

By the way...

Same-sex partnerships in Japan

Currently (in 2019), same-sex marriage is not legal in Japan, but 24 local governments issue certificates to recognize "relationships equivalent to marriage." Shibuya, Tokyo began issuing partnership certificates in November 2015, along with the neighboring municipality of Setagaya. Nagoya hasn't followed suit yet...

23 カナダと日本、イヌの飼い方もちがう

わが家は5人と1匹。ヨークシャーテリアのジローを、手放さざるを得なかった前の飼い主からひきつぎ1年。来た当初はスリムだったのに、いまの飼い主に似てメタボ腹。

私が名古屋に住んでいた90年代、瀬戸市に住んでいた義理の両親は、柴犬のアトムと黒い雑種のルビーを飼っていました。2匹はいつも庭にいました。日本では犬を外で飼っている家庭が多いことに気づき、カナダとちがうなぁと思いました。家の中では靴をぬぐ文化の日本で、清潔さを保つためでしょうか。カナダでは、寒さに強いハスキー犬でも、家の中で飼うのが一般的です。

97年に結婚後、当時私は学生で、語学教師もしていたため、妻とはライフスタイルがずれていました。さみしく感じた妻は、給料ひと月ぶんをはたいて犬を飼ったのです。売れ残っていたボストンテリアをセール価格でゲット。

当時でも、大金をだしてペットを買うことにびっくりしたのですが、いまではそのころの倍くらいの価格にさらにびっくり。新しい家族になったブチャカワ「ショコラ」はペットブームのさきがけで（勝手に思っているのですが）、そのころから日本中に小型犬がはやりだし、ブランド意識が強くなっていったように思います。

ショコラがやってきてほどなく、99年に生まれた娘は、ショコラと大

さくらとジロー
Sakura and Jiro

の仲良し。だけど残念なことに、湿疹（しっしん）だらけの長女は当時、犬のアレルギーがあると判明したのです。悩んだ末、義理の両親がひきとってくれました。

私の住まいの近所には動物病院が２つ、ペット美容室は３店もあります。ドッグフードはもちろん、おやつも種類が豊富で、カットに洋服にと、現代の日本の犬たちは室内で優雅な生活を送っていますね。

ラサール領事のおまけ話

カナダではイヌ派が増加中？

カナダでは近年、ネコを飼う人口があまり変わらないのに対し、イヌを飼う人が増え続けています。2018年現在で、イヌは820万匹、ネコは830万匹がペットとして飼われていて、イヌを飼う家庭は全体の41％、ネコを飼う家庭は全体の38％です。（カナダ動物衛生研究所しらべ）

23 Keeping pets in Canada and Japan

Our family: 5 people, 1 dog. Yorkshire Terrier Jiro joined our household about a year ago after his previous owners had to part with him. A very slim little dog when we got him, Jiro has since put on quite a bit of weight around his waist, which makes him look a little like his master (me).

When I lived in Nagoya back in the 90s, my in-laws in Seto had two dogs, a Shiba ken called Atom and a black mixed breed called Ruby. Both were always in their backyard. I noticed that many Japanese did the same and kept their dogs in the backyard. Hum, that's different from Canada, I thought to myself. Japanese people remove their shoes before entering a home, so maybe it was for similar reasons of cleanliness? In Canada, even Huskies, who are very resistant to the cold, are normally kept inside the home.

When we got married in 1997, I was still a student at Nagoya University and I also taught English and French part time. Our schedules didn't match, so my wife decided to buy herself some company and put up one full month's salary on a dog. She got a great deal on a "leftover" Boston Terrier.

At the time, I was very surprised that she would pay that much for a dog but I was even more surprised when I noticed that in today's Japan, people will pay more than twice that amount for dogs! At any

rate, our "so ugly he's cute" 'Chocolat' was a trend-setting pioneer (in my book!) for the "pet boom" that would later sweep the country. In the years that followed, small dogs gradually became popular in Japan and pedigree became more important.

Not long after Chocolat joined our household, we greeted the arrival of our first daughter, Sakura in 1999. Sakura and Chocolat got along marvelously but unfortunately, our daughter developed rashes on her body caused by an allergic reaction to the dog. We were left with no other choice than to let him go and the in-laws in Seto took him in.

In my neighborhood, there are 2 veterinarians and 3 pet "salons". Dog food, even dog treats are available in many varieties. Dogs get haircuts and wear dog clothes. Today's Japanese dogs get to live a life of comfort inside the house!

By the way...

10 most popular dog breeds in Japan (2019)

According to pet insurance company, Anicom,

1.Toy Poodle 2.Chihuahua 3.Mixed-breed(under 10kg)
4.Shiba-inu 5.Mini Dachshund 6.Pomeranian 7.Mini Schnauzer
8.Yorkshire Terrier 9.Shih Tzu 10.French Bulldog

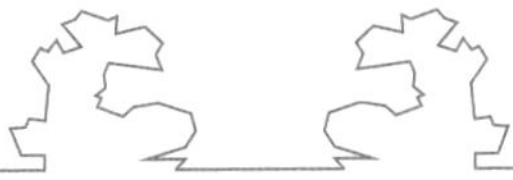

24 カナダ領事のペットフレンドリーな旅

2019年の夏は家族旅行の行き先をどこにしようかと考えたとき、いつもは瀬戸の妻の実家でお留守番しているヨークシャーテリアのジローをつれていける場所をさがしました。いざ、蓼科（たてしな）へ！　宿泊は、小型犬同伴ＯＫのペンション。

ドライブでの旅は、高速道路はパパ、市内はママがハンドルをにぎります（公平にね！）。名古屋を出発して、まずは長野県の諏訪湖（すわこ）へ。陸からそのまま湖にダイブして浮かぶという水陸両用バスに乗って、諏訪の観光スポットを周遊しました。その後、雄大な景色を楽しみながら、ペンションに到着。荷物をおいたら、まずはジローの散歩。

夕食の時間、となりのテーブルの夫婦の横には２匹の小さな犬たち

長野にて
左からママ、ジローを抱えた太朗、ももこ

Noriko, Momoko and Taro holding Jiro in Nagano

（ウィペット）が、おとなしくイスに座っていました。スゴイ！！　食いしん坊のジローには到底無理なので、部屋でお留守番。ほかと比較してはいけません、私たちはジローのありのままが好きなのです。

ペンションのオーナー夫婦は名古屋出身で、犬をつれていける観光地やレストランをいろいろとすすめてくれました。思った以上に、ペットをつれていけるところが多いのにおどろきました。

ジローはボートや、ケーブルカーにも乗れ、牧場、森林の中のアスレチック、遊園地にも行けたのです。今や３世帯に１世帯はペットを飼っているご時世で、一番の問題は旅行に行けないことです。蓼科のようにペットフレンドリーな観光地は本当に助かります。

この旅でジローが興奮したのはミニゴルフでした。彼はボール遊びが大好きなのです。私たちは、ジローがボールを追いかけないように見張っていなくてはなりませんでした…（ちなみに、その試合は私が勝ちました）。

さて、こまったこともありました。当のジローは、環境の変化のせいか、ふだんは快食快便の健康犬が、なんと便秘になってしまったのです。交代で何度も散歩につれていったのですが、なかなか成果は出ず。滞在３日目にしてようやくいつものジローに戻れました。犬のちょっとした『介護』も、ペットフレンドリーな旅の思い出のひとつです。

ラサール領事のおまけ話

ペットにやさしいカナダの街

カナダの街は概してペットにやさしく、飼い犬のリードをはずして自由に走りまわらせることのできる「リード不要」の公園もたくさんあります。もちろんペットの安全は、飼い主が責任をもって守らなければいけませんけれどね。

24 The Canadian Consul's pet-friendly vacation

When the family goes on a trip, we normally leave our Yorkshire Terrier Jiro behind with the in-laws in Seto but this summer, we decided to look for a pet-friendly destination so that Jiro could join the rest of the family on vacation. We found such a place in Tateshina. Our accommodations: a pet friendly inn.

When the family goes on a road trip, Dad (me) handles the highway driving and Mom grabs the steering wheel in the city (fair is fair!). Our first stop, Lake Suwa in Nagano prefecture where we boarded an amphibious bus that can travel on land and water, and on which we got to see all the sites that Suwa has to offer. Then we drove to our inn while admiring the striking scenery. After dropping off our luggage in our room, it was time for Jiro's walk.

At dinnertime that evening, the couple sitting at the table next to ours had company. They were joined by their two small dogs (whippets?) who were both perched very quietly on a chair next to their owners. Quite impressive! Our little Jiro loves food too much, so there's no way he could be so well-behaved during the meal so we left him in the room. But it's best not to compare Jiro with other dogs, we love him just the way he is...

The couple who ran the inn were from Nagoya and they were nice enough to recommend many pet-friendly locations and restaurants

in the region. I was pleasantly surprised by the number of places that allow dogs. Our Jiro was able to join us on boats, in a gondola, at a farm, in the forest for some hiking, and even in an amusement park. In Japan, where one in three households now owns a pet, going on vacation has become problematic, so pet-friendly places like Tateshina are really a great option.

The part of our trip that got Jiro most excited was the round of mini golf we played. Jiro loves to play fetch so we all had to keep an eye on him so he didn't run after our golf balls... (I won the game, by the way!)

Now we did encounter one small problem during the trip. The complete change of environment was making our Jiro nervous and our little guy - who is normally very "regular" - was having a bout of constipation. The family took turns taking him on many extra walks every day hoping he would get better but nothing worked. On the third day of the trip, he was finally able to "do his thing". "Nursing" our dog, one of the many memories from our pet friendly trip to Nagano...

By the way...

Where is Tateshina?

Tateshina is a highland in Nagano prefecture, offering a view of Mount Tateshina to the North and the Yatsugatake Mountains to the East. It's about 2 hours by train or car from Nagoya. It's a popular destination in summer to get away from the heat and enjoy some lovely alpine scenery!

25 尾鷲の移住体験、いいね

名古屋のカナダ領事館に着任して最初の公式訪問地は三重県尾鷲市でした。当時の岩田昭人市長から、カナダのプリンスルパート市との姉妹提携記念植樹祭への家族招待をうけました。わざわざ名古屋まで車をとばして会いにきてくれた熱意に私は心を打たれ、妻は世界遺産にも登録された熊野古道のハイキングにたいへん乗り気で、即ゴーサインが出ました。

名古屋からバスで４時間。尾鷲に到着して、私が最初に気づいたのは、バス停のすぐそばに立つ大きな病院でした。そして、ナイスロケーション！　海と山の豊かな自然にめぐまれた地でした。

熊野古道センターの広場でおこなわれた植樹祭では、市長をはじめ、家族皆シャベルを手にし、プリンスルパートの州花であるハナミズキを植えました。この子たちが大人になり、成長した木を見にまた尾鷲を訪れるはずだと思ったのでした。

その後、市長に人口についてたずねると、一番多いときは３万人で、現在は１万８千人に減ったとのこと。出生率の低下はカナダも同様で、ある州では助成金を投じて保育園のほぼ無料化をはかるなど、家族を支援するさまざまな社会政策を実行しています。カナダは移民うけいれにたいへん積極的なので、日本ほど人口問題は深刻ではありません。

ももこ、熊野古道にて

Momoko on the Kumanokodo trail

尾鷲では人々を呼びこむ対策に力を入れているそうです。そのひとつに移住体験住宅プログラムがあります。尾鷲に長期的にコミットする前に、短期的な滞在をサポートする対策です。なるほど、市民になる前の「おためし住宅」ですね。あのバス停そばの大きな病院について、まちの魅力のひとつではないですかというと、市長は「24時間、年中無休ですよ」と即座(そくざ)にアピール。

翌日、私たちは熊野古道を歩き、たくさんの思い出とともに尾鷲を離れました。妻も私も、こういう小さなまちは「訪れる」だけでしたが、「住む」のも悪くないとうなずきあったのでした。それは、もう少し年をとってから「体験」してもいいかも。海とハイキングを楽しみ、そしてまさかのときにはあの立派な病院で。

ラサール領事のおまけ話

カナダでも高齢化の波

カナダでも2014年に、65歳以上の人口が、総人口の15.6%にあたる600万人を超えました。あと20年と経たない2030年には、カナダの高齢者人口は950万人を超え、総人口の23%を占めると考えられています。

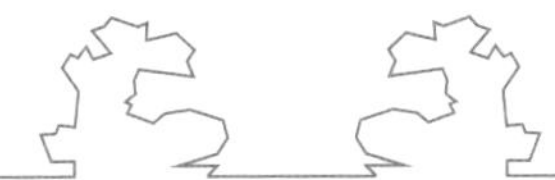

25 Moving to Owase on a "trial basis"

The very first official visit I received after becoming Consul in Nagoya was from the city of Owase in Mie prefecture. The mayor and a delegation of about 4 people had driven all the way to Nagoya to invite me to a tree planting ceremony to commemorate the twinning of their city with Prince Rupert in Canada. I was touched by the fact that they had come all this way to invite me. My wife, on the other hand, loved the idea of hiking on the UNESCO World Heritage Kumanokodo trail. It's official, we're going on a family trip!

It was a 4-hour bus ride to Owase. The first thing I noticed upon my arrival was the surprisingly big hospital right next to the bus stop. Second thing I noticed was the nice location! Owase is surrounded by nature, with the sea on one side and some lush green mountains on the other.

With shovel in hand, the whole family joined the mayor at the Kumanokodo Center plaza to plant a Pacific Dogwood, the official flower (and tree) of British Columbia, the province where Prince Rupert is located. I'm sure the kids will revisit Owase later in life to get another look at "their" tree.

Later in the day, I asked the mayor about the city's population. The mayor answered that it now stood at about 18,000 but added that at its peak it had been around 30,000. Low birthrates are a problem in

Canada as well and various levels of government responded with a mix of social policies to support families – like heavily subsidized day care in certain provinces. Canada is also very welcoming of immigration, which means population renewal is not as acute a problem as it is in Japan.

Owase had its own initiatives to attract new residents. One of their programs allowed people to come and live in Owase on a "trial basis" to see if they like it before committing to stay there for the long run. I get it, it's a new twist on the "try before you buy" approach to marketing. I told the mayor I had noticed the nice hospital at the bus stop and I added that it must be part of the enticement package to attract new residents. The mayor nodded and quickly added, "it's open 24/7, 365 days a year!"

We went hiking on the Kumanokodo trail the next day and left the city full of memories. For my wife and me, small cities were generally just places to "visit" but when we talked about Owase, we both agreed we could probably "live" there. Maybe on a "trial basis" when we're a bit older. Seafood and hiking every day, with a nice hospital just in case...

By the way...

Japan, the world's "oldest" country

In 2019, over 35 million Japanese are aged 65 or older, representing 28.4 percent of the country's population, the highest percentage in the world. By 2030—in less than two decades—seniors will number over 37 million and make up 31 percent of the Japanese population.

26 カナダ領事、ムズムズする

先日、あいち航空ミュージアムから帰る途中、偶然にも昔住んでいた勝川駅近くのアパートの前を通りすぎました。97年に結婚して、最初に住んだところです。選んだ理由は、通勤に便利でわりと安かったから。近年、JRセントラルタワーズやミッドランドスクエアといった名古屋駅の再開発により、勝川駅周辺もめざましい成長をとげました。

2001年に春日井から東京へ引っ越しました。私も妻も東京は未知の街。知人のすすめで、交通の便がよく、それほど高くない地区という条件で、東急東横線沿線の武蔵小杉駅の近くに住むことになりました。その後、04年に私たちが日本を離れると、同駅周辺は急速に発展し、いまではタワーマンションがたちならぶ人気の住宅エリアです。

さて、カナダに帰国してアルバータ州政府で働きはじめて半年がすぎたころ、なぜだかわかりませんが、家を買うことばかりが頭をよぎり、なにかにせかされるように、私たち家族にとっては初の一軒家を購入しました。石油が豊富にとれるアルバータ州は当時、石油価格の急上昇で不動産も高騰していました。もう少し遅かったら、手がとどかなかったはずです。こうしてふりかえってみると、私には不動産に先見の明があるのかも？　残念ながら、私の意外な才能はいかせず、持ち家は売ってしまいました。

仕事がら、引っ越しばかりで家をもつことはむずかしいのですが、

名古屋に住みはじめて２年たったところから、ムズムズがはじまりました。愛知は元気がいいし、発展し続けています。妻の故郷で、私が学生生活をすごした場所でもある愛知に、家がほしいなあと思うようになったのです。退職後は大須に小さいマンションってのもいいなあ。義理の家族の住む瀬戸もいいかも。再び春日井もいいなあ。雑誌を読むように、インターネットで物件を見ては想像をふくらませるのは楽しいですね。

ラサール領事のおまけ話

カナダの不動産価格の高い街ベスト10（2019）

1. トロント　7593万円（$921,000）　2. バンクーバー　7242万円（$878,242）
3. カルガリー　4700万円（$570,084）　4. エドモントン　3188万円（$378,247）
5. オタワ　3077万円（$373,200）　6. モントリオール　2877万円（$349,000）
7. レジーナ　2613万円（$316,990）　8. ハリファックス　2530万円（$306,944）
9. ウィニペグ　2473万円（$300,011）　10. ケベック　2198万円（$266,578）

※戸建ての家の平均価格　※$はカナダドル
(出典 : worldatlas.com 2019)

26 The Canadian Consul's itch...

On the way back from the Aichi Museum of Flight, we happened to drive by an apartment near Kachigawa station where we used to live. It was the first place my wife and I lived together after we got married in 1997. We had chosen that area for convenience – and because it was relatively cheap. Since then, new developments around Nagoya Station, such as the JR Central Towers and Midland Square, have spurred tremendous growth around Kachigawa station.

My wife and I left Kasugai in 2001 and moved to Tokyo. Neither of us had ever lived in Tokyo. Our family's criteria were the same: an easy commute and not too expensive. A friend recommended the Musashi Kosugi area along the Toyoko line so that's where we moved. Our family left Japan a few years later in 2004. Interestingly, not long after our departure, new developments started to sprout like mushrooms around Musashi Kosugi station and it has become a very popular residential area filled with high-rise apartment buildings.

After the family moved back to Canada, I started working for the provincial government of Alberta. I don't know why, but within 6 months of our arrival, I suddenly got a strong urge to buy property. And that's what we did, our young family bought its very first home. The province of Alberta is rich in oil and at that very moment, the price of oil started to rise quickly – and so did the price of real estate!

If we had waited much longer before buying, home ownership would have quickly become unaffordable for us. Looking back on our real estate history, I couldn't help but think that, maybe, we had a special real estate "foretelling" talent? Unfortunately, I was never able to exploit that talent fully and we sold our house in Canada before coming back to Japan.

Moving from place to place is now part of my job as a diplomat and that's making home ownership more complicated for our family. But we've been in Nagoya for 2 years now and the "itch" is back. Aichi is a dynamic region that continues to grow. It's also where my wife grew up and where I spent a big part of my student days. Maybe we could buy a home here? A small apartment near Osu, my favorite part of Nagoya? Or maybe a house in Seto near the in-laws? We could go back to Kasugai? Like turning the pages of a glossy magazine, it's just fun to dream a little while searching for property on the internet.

By the way...

The most popular place to live in Japan

According to web based real estate agency SUUMO, in 2019, Yokohama was the most popular place to live for Japanese people aged 20-49. In western Japan, Nishinomiya in Hyogo was the most popular. Nagoya wasn't included in either eastern nor western Japan in this survey, but another agency, Nissho, did identify the most popular areas in Nagoya. They were: 1.Sakae 2.Hoshigaoka 3.around Nagoya station

27 カナダ領事は事故物件でも大丈夫？

そんなこんなで、妻の故郷であり、好景気な愛知県にマイホームがほしいと思うようになってきました。退職までもうちょっとあるし、この先引っ越しもあるだろうから、すぐには住めないけど、貸してもいいのだし…というわけで物件さがしがはじまりました。

まずは場所選び。お気にいりの大須はもちろん、地下鉄東山線沿線、妻の両親が住んでいる瀬戸に近い藤が丘、あるいは八事…。物件をさがすのにインターネット検索エンジンはベストですね。写真とともに、場所、広さ、築年数など必要な情報が満載。数ある中からおもしろそうな中古マンション６件を選びました。

春日井では
こんな物件で
暮らしていました

Stopping by our old apartment in Kasugai – time flies!

内見を手配してくれる不動産業者を見つけるため、インターネットで名前と電話番号を入力して「送信」をクリック。数分後には不動産業者から連絡。なんて速い！数時間後、興味深いメッセージをうけとりました。お気にいり物件のひとつに「過去」があるというのです。「前の所有者はおフロで死亡」。でも事件ではなく「自然死」。しかし「リフォーム済みのため、おフロも新品」。最後に「それでも訪問したいですか？」。

私の最初の反応は「？」。人はどこかで死ぬ。それがおフロなら、平和なことじゃないか。しかし、不動産業者が告知するぐらいなのだから、日本人の中には難色を示す人がいるようですね。カナダでは、自然死を小さなこととして誰も気にしません。私は問題のマンションを「それでも見たい」とつたえました。結果は、とてもよいマンションでした（新しいおフロもきれいでしたし）。しかし、駅からはちょっと離れた場所だったため却下。私の完璧なマイホーム探しの旅は、続く。

ラサール領事のおまけ話

事故物件も程度により

この記事を書いてから、日本には「事故物件」を紹介するウェブサイトがたくさんあることを知り、おどろきました。カナダではその物件で誰かが亡くなったとしても、自然死であれば、気にする人はほとんどいません。ただ、さすがに凶悪犯罪が起こった物件となれば、私もほとんどのカナダ人も、買うのをためらうでしょう…。

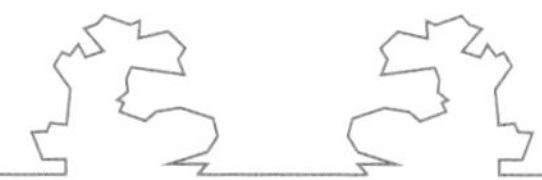

27 Is the Canadian Consul fine with a property "with a past"?

In the end, my wife and I both agreed that it felt right to buy a property in Aichi, her dynamic and prosperous home prefecture. I'm still quite a few years from retirement and there are likely more international moves on the horizon for our family so we don't need an Aichi home for ourselves right now, but we could rent it out... and so, our search for the right property started!

First, we had to choose the area. Of course, there's Osu that I love... Or we could look along the Higashiyama Line, maybe Fujigaoka with its easy access to Seto where my wife's parents live? Or maybe in Yagoto? The best way to search for property is with an internet search engine. The info is all there, location, size, year of construction with lots of pictures. I picked out about 6 properties that looked interesting.

Next, I needed an agent who could help arrange visits. The internet again. I just typed in my name, phone number, and clicked on "send". Just a few minutes later an agent rang us up to offer her services – very quick! A few hours later, I got a rather interesting message from the agent. Apparently, one of the properties on my list had a "past". "The previous owner died in his bath" she wrote, adding that it was a "natural death (not violent)". Finally, she said "the house has been fully

renovated so it has a new bath". She asked if I still wanted to visit.

The question struck me as odd. It did not matter to me at all. People die in their homes all the time, and dying in your bath sounds like a peaceful way to go, right? But it seems that quite a few people in Japan worry about these things; so much so that the agent felt some obligation to inform me. Back home in Canada, no one would care about a natural death. I told the agent I still wanted to see the apartment in question. It was actually pretty nice (and the new bath was nice too) but it was a bit far from the station so we passed. Our search for the perfect property continues...

By the way...

Depends on the "problem"...

Since I wrote this article, I was surprised to find out there are many websites in Japan that help people identify "problem properties" (jiko bukken). In Canada, very few people would be bothered by property where someone passed away under normal circumstances. However, I have to admit I would balk at buying property that was the scene of a horrible crime – and I'm sure many Canadians would feel the same way.

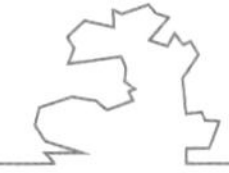

28 カナダ領事のケッタ通勤

90年代にカナダから来た私がおどろいたことのひとつは、自転車に乗る人が多いことです。カナダではアウトドアスポーツとして、夏になるとよく見かけます。道幅のせまい日本では、1年を通じて、移動や買いものなどの運搬手段として使っているのですね。

2016年に再来日したのは、猛暑の8月。家から駅までの汗だくの15分の徒歩通勤は、ママチャリをゲットして、爽快な5分となりました。そして、私が日本を離れていた12年の間に、自転車の交通ルールも変わったことに気づきました。

昔は、歩道でも自転車がわがもの顔で通行していました。うしろから、「チャリン、チャリン」と鳴らされ、ビックリさせられたこともしばしば。今は子どもや高齢者をのぞいて、自転車は車道を走ることが求められ、ほとんどの人が新しい規則を尊重しています。カサさし運転も違法。

自転車に乗る私
Me on my bike

ほかにも、名古屋では駅前に駐輪場が設置されているため、ごったがえしの自転車の山から、自分のケッタをさがさなくてもいいし、景観も損なわれません。

かわったのは、規則だけではありませんでした。私が住む地域は坂が多く、駅まではのぼり坂が多いので、朝から気合をいれないと、たどりつけません。一番軽いギアにして、息をきらして自転車をこいでいる私を横目に、おばちゃん（中年の女性）がスイスイと私を追いぬいていくではありませんか。（ワォ〜！どういうこと？）私は、少し落ちこみました。ところが、おなじことが次の日も、また別の日も起こったのです。なにかおかしい…。信号待ちで、となりの自転車をよく見てみると、ペダルのすぐ上のサドル下のフレームになにか箱がついているのです。わかったぞ！バッテリーだ！私ははじめて、電動アシスト自転車を目にしたのです。そして、自分の運動不足が原因ではなかったことにホッとしました。そりゃ、負けるさ。毎朝の坂道レースはフェアレースじゃないんだもの。

私も「電動クラブ」の一員になろうかという考えが頭をよぎりましたが、やっぱり参加しないことにしました。どうせわが家の財務大臣はOKしてくれないだろうし、メタボ解消に坂道エクササイズは必要なのです！

ラサール領事のおまけ話

故郷の自転車が日本で大人気！

2016年に再来日して、街中にルイガノの自転車があることにおどろきました。ルイガノは私の故郷・ケベックの自転車ブランドです。私が20代のころ、カナダでもルイガノのサイクリング用ヘルメットが大流行しました。日本で販売されているルイガノの自転車は、ライセンス契約のもと、日本国内で製造されています。

28 The Canadian Consul rides his bike to work

When I first came to Japan in the 90s, one of the things that struck me was how popular bicycles were as a daily mode of transportation. In Canada, bikes are popular as an outdoor sport and you see a lot of them in the summer months. In crowded Japanese cities, they are a great way to travel the short distance from home to the closest subway station or supermarket throughout the year.

Our family returned to Japan in August 2016. The scorching Nagoya summer was a good reason to commute by bike: my "sweaty" 15-minute walk to the subway station turned into a more "breezy" 5-minute bike ride.

I also noticed that Japanese bicycle "etiquette" had changed during my 12-year absence. I remember that in the past, cyclists in Japan would ride on the sidewalk like they owned it! The constant "charin" (the Japanese onomatopoeia for bicycle bells) of cyclists wanting you to get out of their way made walking sidewalks a stressful experience. But the rules have changed in Nagoya and except for kids and seniors, cyclists are now expected to keep to the roads and most people respect the new rules. It's also illegal to ride your bike with an umbrella in hand.

Another change is the bicycle parking lots near subway stations. This solves the problem of having to find your bike in a pile of

entangled metal – it's also less of an eyesore.

But etiquette is not the only thing that's changed. The area around my house is full of hills so it's quite a challenge to get to the station every morning. I remember riding to the station in first gear huffing and puffing up the hill when another cyclist, a middle-aged woman, just whizzed passed me. Wow. She made it look so effortless! I blamed myself: "I must be out of shape". But the same scene was repeated twice in the next few days. Something was off... When we were stopped at a red light, I took a closer look at one of these strangely fast bikes and noticed that there was a thick block attached to the frame just above the pedals. I get it, it's a battery for a motor that powers the bike! That's when I discovered electric power assisted bicycles. I was relieved that my health wasn't the problem. No wonder! They weren't playing by the same rules!

I'll admit that I considered joining the "electric club" but decided against it. I knew my finance minister (my wife) wouldn't approve the purchase - and my middle-aged heart needed a regular hill climbing work out!

By the way...

Canadian bikes are now popular in Japan!

When I returned to Japan in 2016, I was surprised to see so many "Louis Garneau" bikes on the roads in Nagoya. Louis Garneau comes from my home province of Quebec and I remember that when I was in my twenties, Louis Garneau cycling helmets were all the rage in Canada. The Louis Garneau bikes sold in Japan are made in Japan under a branding agreement.

29 カナダ領事のバス通勤

おはずかしいのですが、最近、私はギプス生活を余儀なくされました。ごく自然なことですが、周囲の視線はギプスに注がれます。スキーや柔道の練習中なんて理由なら、ちょっとカッコイイのですが、実際は慣れない靴で階段をふみはずしただけなのです。痛みはそれほどなかったのですが、足の甲が日ごとに青くなってゆくので、病院へ。全治1カ月の骨折と診断。

ギプスのおかげで東京、大阪への出張もキャンセル。とはいえ、仕事にはいかなくてはいけません。駅までの自転車は、この足では無理。歩いてもいけないし、運転もできません。妻も仕事があるので、迷惑はかけたくありません。

すると、同僚が家の近くのバス停からオフィスのすぐ目の前に停まるルートを調べてくれました。乗りかえもなく、一本でオフィス近くまでいけるのです。ワオ～、知らなかった！

バス通勤初日。
松葉づえが不便で
すぐにやめる

First day on the bus.
I did't like crutches
and stopped using
them the next day

名古屋には、名大生だったころから数えて10年以上住んでいるのに、バスに乗ったことはありませんでした。ですから、バスの乗り方をイチから学ばなくては。市バスは前乗り、後ろ降りの先払いですが、私が乗る基幹２号は後ろ乗り、前降りの後払い。マナカ OK のどこまで乗っても一律 210 円。運行時間も朝は６分おき、帰りは 10 分おきと、意外と便利。へぇ～、すこしだけ早起きすれば、地下鉄よりも安いし、景色も見られてちょっと楽しいかも。ただ、バス前面の系統名と行き先はよ～く確認すること！（１度だけちがう行き先のバスに乗ってしまって、妻の過密スケジュールを乱すことになり、激怒されました）

私はなるべく優先席を避（さ）けます。松葉づえなしでいると私のギプスに気づかない人もいるので、優先席にすわる外国人を不快に思う人がいるかもしれません。私はカナダ領事であると同時に「ガイジン大使」でもあるので、外国人として好印象を得られるようにつとめています。

とにもかくにも、このバス通勤は偶然のうれしい発見でした。でも、たったひとつだけ惜（お）しい！所があります。それは、バスの座席に私の足が収まらないことです（自慢のつもりではありませんよ）。最近では、きちんと足を座席に収める方法もマスターしました。ギプスがとれたあとも、バス通勤を続けようかな…。

ラサール領事のおまけ話

都市によって公共交通機関の使い方も違う

これまで世界のさまざまな都市で暮らしてきて、街によって公共交通機関に対する考え方もちがうことに気がつきました。モントリオールや、北米東海岸の人口密集地である「古い街」では、公共交通機関は多くの人にとっての生活の足であり、マイカーを持つ余裕のある人でも、便利だからと公共交通機関を利用します。しかし、カナダ西部のエドモントンや、アメリカ南部のヒューストンのような新興都市では、車に乗ることが「ステータス」のようになっていて、公共交通機関を避けて、マイカーでの長～い通勤にわざわざ耐えています。日本はというと、東京、大阪、名古屋のような大都市では、経済状況にかかわらず、地下鉄やバスを利用するのがしごく合理的なようです。いいね！

29 The Canadian Consul takes the bus

O.K. O.K. I goofed up and now I have to walk with a cast on my leg. You see casts all the time but they do catch people's attention and then come the questions... I wish I had a cool story to tell, maybe a ski accident or even better Judo? But no, it was a pair of new shoes that were too tight and a misstep going down the stairs... It didn't hurt that much but the bruise under my foot kept getting darker every day so eventually I went to the hospital. The diagnosis: a fracture that would take a month to heal.

I had to cancel 2 business trips, one to Tokyo and another to Osaka. But I still had to show up at work. I usually ride my bike to the subway station but cycling was now impossible. Walking to the station was also impossible and since it was my right foot that was injured, driving to work wasn't possible either... I couldn't ask my wife to become my chauffeur for a month – she has obligations at work so I couldn't disrupt her schedule too much.

One of my colleagues told me about a bus stop not far from my house and one of the buses that ran from there had a stop directly in front of my office. No transfers, nothing – same bus straight to the office! Wow, I didn't even know.

I'd lived a total of 10 years in Nagoya (7 years in the 90s and 3 years since I became consul in 2016) but I don't think I had taken the bus a single time. So I had to learn everything from scratch even the small things like where to get on – in the middle on the "kikan buses" I rode; and when to pay – when getting off at the front of the bus. I can use my rechargeable "Manaca" smart card and

the fee is 210 yen no matter the distance. The times were also very convenient with buses running every 6 minutes in the morning and every 10 minutes in the evening. Surprisingly convenient. I would have to get up just a bit earlier, but it's cheaper than the subway and I could enjoy the scenery on the way to work. Could be fun. One piece of advice though, make sure you get on the right bus! (I got on the wrong bus once and it wreaked havoc on my wife's tight schedule. My wife was not pleased…)

Even if there are reserved seats in the middle of the bus for "injured" people like me, I avoid them. Without crutches, people don't always notice that my leg is hurt so they might think I'm abusing. I'm the Canadian consul but I'm also the "Gaijin (foreigner) ambassador", so I want to make a good impression…

At any rate, the Nagoya bus system turned out to be a pleasant discovery. There's only one small drawback I can think of: it's hard to fit my long legs in the back seat (I'm not bragging!) But somehow, I've learned how to fold them neatly under the seat. Nagoya buses just might become a daily part of my routine even after my cast is removed…

By the way...

Attitudes towards public transit

I've lived in many cities around the world and I've noticed that attitudes towards public transit vary greatly from city to city. In Montreal and other densely populated "older cities" on the East coast of North America, public transit is used by a cross section of the population and even affluent people who could afford a car will use public transit because it's convenient. In younger cities like Edmonton in western Canada and in Houston in the southern US, traveling by car is a "status thing" meaning that some people frown public transit – preferring to endure ridiculously long commutes in their car rather than riding a bus... And in Japan? In big cities like Tokyo, Osaka and Nagoya, rich or poor, it just makes sense to use the subway or bus - and that's a good thing!

30 名古屋は「家族にやさしい街(まち)」

家族旅行でディズニーリゾートにいってきました。私にとっては、約14年ぶりのディズニーランドでしたが、USJに行ったときのように、外国人の来場者の多さに気づくと同時に、日本にとって、外国からの観光客がどれほど重要であるかを考えさせられました。

では、ここ名古屋に外国人観光客をいかに誘致(ゆうち)するか。地元にねざした戦略「家族にやさしい都市」で勝負したほうがいいと思います。

そのひとつは、なんといってもレゴランド。子どもだけでなく大人もハマるレゴブロックは、家族で楽しめる高品質のブランドです。長久手市のトヨタ博物館を訪れたときも、おどろきました。「ワオ！本物の三輪メッサーシュミットだ、あちらは本物のドラージュ D8-120だ！」。ふだん写真でしか見られない名車のオンパレードですよ。つい最近オープンしたあいち航空ミュージアムでは世界的に有名なゼロ戦をはじめ、歴史的な飛行機を間近で見ることができます。自動車や飛行機はとってもクールで、こうした施設は産業のまち、名古屋の魅力をもっと身近に「家族」につたえることができます。

さらに、ジブリパークは楽しみですね。子どもだけでなく、ジブリ映画で育った中年世代にとっても完成が待ち遠しいですね。世界中でも人気があるジブリ映画ですから、海外からの観光客もおおいに期待できます。

まだまだあります。復元された名古屋城本丸御殿（ごてん）を訪れ、大須に足をのばせば、名古屋の歴史や文化の魅力を堪能（たんのう）できるのです。

名古屋という街は、本当に「家族にやさしい」旅行先なのです。そして、名古屋が東京と大阪に勝っているものが他にもあります。外国人観光客にとって「親しみやすい」、つまり「フレンドリー」ということです。次話で名古屋が観光名所として「かしこい」武器をもつことについてもっとお話しします。

ラサール領事のおまけ話

セカンドラン・シアター

名古屋にないなあと思うのが（日本全体にいえることですが）封切りから数カ月後の映画を安い値段で再上映する「セカンドラン・シアター」。カナダやアメリカで暮らした街の多くにこのセカンドラン・シアターがあり、子どもたちとよく映画を観にいったものでした。夫婦でふらっと、夜のデートに出かけるにも恰好の行き先でした。

30 Family friendly Nagoya

Our family recently went on vacation to a Disney resort in Tokyo. I hadn't been to Disneyland in about 14 years, and, just as I did during my trip to USJ back in 2016, I quickly noticed that many of the faces in the crowd were not Japanese. There again, I was witnessing first-hand how important foreign tourism had become to Japan.

Which raises the question: How can Nagoya get its fair share of foreign tourists? Nagoya needs a strategy rooted in its own character; I think Nagoya could brand itself as the "family friendly city".

Legoland could play a central role in this effort. Lego blocks have a high quality "family friendly" image with broad appeal among kids and adults. The Toyota Automobile Museum in Nagakute is another interesting attraction and I was very impressed by the variety of cars in their collection when I visited. "Wow, an actual Messerschmitt 3-wheeler! And over there, a real-life Delage D8-120", dozens and dozens of cars that you generally only see in pictures are all right there in front of you. Another recent addition is the Aichi Museum of Flight where you can get a very close look at many historic airplanes including Japan's world famous "Zero Fighter". Cars and planes are "cool" and have great "family" appeal that could help turn Nagoya's industrial image into something positive.

And you've probably heard that they're going to build a Ghibli

theme park. That'll be a great fun! Kids and their parents - both of whom grew up watching Ghibli movies - are all waiting impatiently for the park to open. Ghibli movies are popular around the world so we can expect foreign fans to flock to Nagoya to visit the park.

But wait, there's more! Visitors could stop by the newly rebuilt annex to Nagoya Castle, and then visit Osu where they can take in some of Nagoya's culture and history.

Nagoya really makes for a "family friendly" trip. But there's another category where Nagoya can beat Tokyo and Osaka: "being friendly" to foreign tourists. I'll tell you more about making "congeniality" a weapon in Nagoya's tourism attraction arsenal in my next column...

By the way...

Second-run theaters

One thing I noticed is missing in Nagoya (and Japan in general) are movie theaters known as "second-run" theaters. These theaters show movies at a reduced price after they leave "first-run" theaters, which is generally a month or two after the movie comes out. There were second-run theaters in many of the cities we lived in, in Canada and the U.S., and we would take the kids there very often. It also made for a great impromptu date night with my wife!

ラサール領事のなごや日記

31 名古屋を フレンドリー大都市へ

東京出張のとき、私は人の多さにいつも疲れはてて帰ってきます。おかげで通勤に使っている名古屋の地下鉄東山線が、快適にさえ感じられるほどです。大都会の人ごみといそがしさは、人々の心の余裕をうばってしまう理由のひとつだと思うのです。

外国からの観光客による経済効果は大きいはずですが、彼らに対して都会の人たちの対応は、ときに冷たいようにうつります。私が関西国際空港への電車にのったとき、外国人観光客が指定席券をもたずに指定席にすわっていたのです。検札にきた車掌さんはその外国人に対して不快な表情をかくすことなく、イライラしているように見えました。実際のところはさだかでありませんが、観光客は指定席券が必要であることを知らなかっただけかもしれませんし、まわりの席もガラガラだったので、私はもう少し丁寧に笑顔で説明をしてあげてもよかったのではないかと思うのです。

私が日本人の妻と北米に住んでいたときには、彼女が外見で現地の人に冷たくされることはめったにありませんでした。しかし、いったん妻がつたない英語で現地の人に話しはじめると、人によっては表情や態度を変えることもあり、一緒にいる私まで不愉快な思いをすることがありました。

名古屋は、日本で「フレンドリーな大都市」になることで、より多く

名古屋のレゴランドで家族みんなと
The whole family at Legoland Japan in Nagoya

の観光客をひきつけられるでしょう。むずかしいことではないですよ。観光客たちが、おみやげいっぱいの大きな買い物袋をかかえて街を歩いているのをよく見かけます。そういう人たちにちょっとだけやさしくしてあげてください。そんなことでよいのです。

慣れない日本へ観光にきている外国人を、笑顔で助けてください。人がやさしいまち、名古屋が根づけば、外国人はかならずここへ戻ってきます。名古屋は「親しみやすい大都市」として信頼されること、まちがいなし！

ラサール領事のおまけ話

名古屋をアジア屈指の観光地に

東京、大阪、北海道、千葉、沖縄は、2018年にアジア太平洋地域で観光客の多かった都市ベスト20（マスターカード社しらべ）にランクインしています。名古屋もいつか、このランキングに加われるでしょうか？ 材料はそろっています。大きくて、楽しくて、安全な街で、飲食店もたくさん。観光スポットも多く、これからも増えるでしょう（ジブリパークとかね！）市民が協力して名古屋を「日本一フレンドリー」な街にすれば、名古屋は堂々とその地位を得ることができると思うのです。

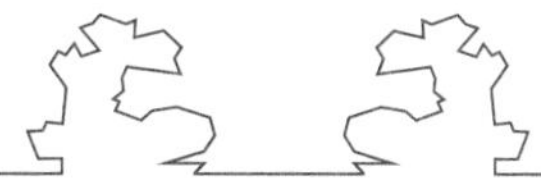

31 Nagoya, the friendly metropolis

Whenever I travel to Tokyo on business, I come back exhausted. But the good thing is that ride on the crowded Higashiyama Line feels almost relaxing when compared to what people in Tokyo have to endure every day. One thing is for sure, the "crushing" experience that is life on the big city ends up robbing us of a bit of our humanity; we become colder.

Foreign tourists clearly have a positive impact on the economy of the cities they visit, but the locals don't always greet them with a smile. I saw it with my own eyes recently. I was on the shuttle that takes people to Kansai International Airport when some foreign tourists sat in the reserved section without tickets. The conductor came by and when he noticed them, he clearly became impatient. No one knows for sure, but there were many empty seats, so maybe these tourists had made an honest mistake? I think the conductor could have been more tactful when dealing with the situation.

When we lived in North America, my Japanese wife was never treated poorly because of her appearance. However, when she starts talking, people quickly understand that she isn't local. Most people were still nice with her but some became impatient and it showed in their tone or their faces, which upset my wife – and her husband as well.

Nagoya could definitely attract more tourists by becoming Japan's "friendly big city". It's actually pretty simple. You often see foreign tourists carrying many bags full of things they bought in Nagoya. Just be nice to those people. That's all!

When you see a tourist having problems understanding the way things work in Japan, don't get angry, just help them out with a smile. If enough people do it, tourists will notice and they'll come back. And Nagoya will be known as the friendly, approachable city!

By the way...

How Nagoya can become a top destination

Tokyo, Osaka, Hokkaido, Chiba, Okinawa were among the 20 most visited destinations in the Asia Pacific region in 2018 (source: Mastercard). Will Nagoya join the list in the coming years? It has all the ingredients: a large, fun and safe city with plenty of restaurants. It already has many attractions and more are on the way in the near future (Ghibli!). If the citizens of Nagoya do their part and make it the "friendliest" city in Japan, I think Nagoya will take its rightful place on the list!

MAP OF NAGOYA

Nagoya is a big city but it's easy to get around.
A big city with a big heart!
名古屋は大都市だけど、東京のように複雑でないので、
交通網も利用しやすい。

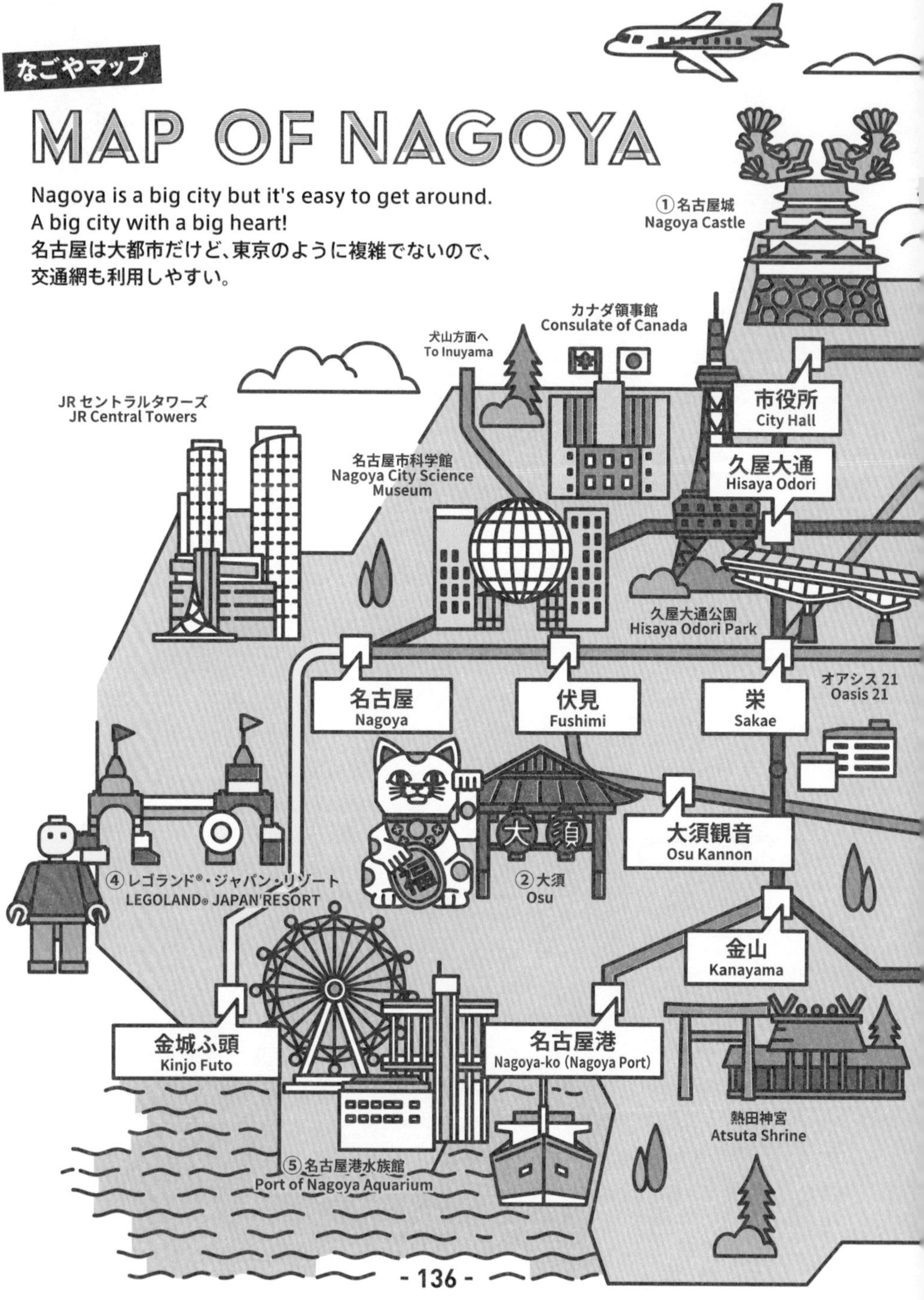

①名古屋城
Nagoya Castle

カナダ領事館
Consulate of Canada

犬山方面へ
To Inuyama

市役所
City Hall

久屋大通
Hisaya Odori

JR セントラルタワーズ
JR Central Towers

名古屋市科学館
Nagoya City Science Museum

久屋大通公園
Hisaya Odori Park

名古屋
Nagoya

伏見
Fushimi

栄
Sakae

オアシス 21
Oasis 21

大須観音
Osu Kannon

④レゴランド®・ジャパン・リゾート
LEGOLAND® JAPAN RESORT

②大須
Osu

金山
Kanayama

金城ふ頭
Kinjo Futo

名古屋港
Nagoya-ko (Nagoya Port)

熱田神宮
Atsuta Shrine

⑤名古屋港水族館
Port of Nagoya Aquarium

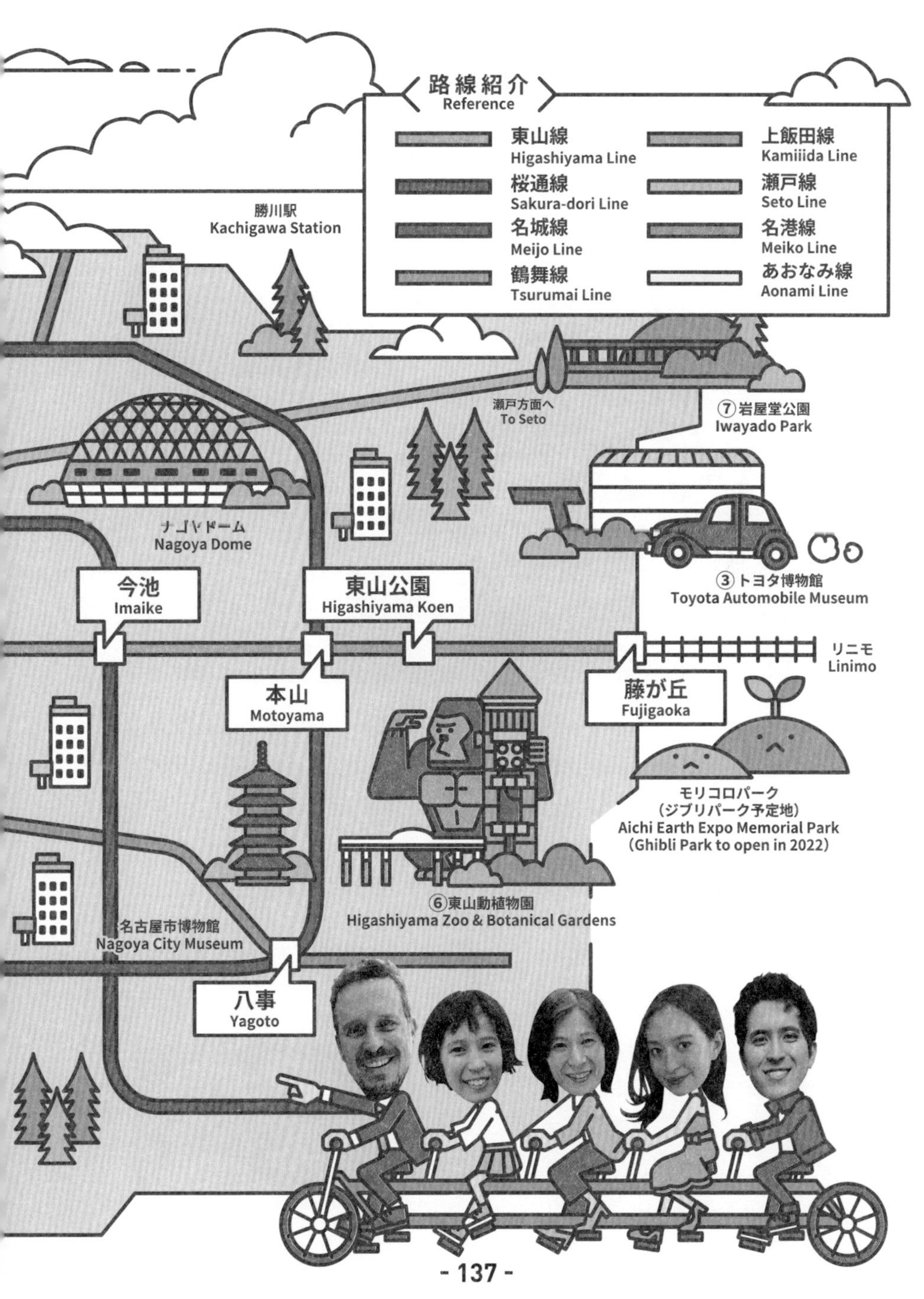

路線紹介
Reference
東山線
Higashiyama Line
上飯田線
Kamiiida Line
桜通線
Sakura-dori Line
瀬戸線
Seto Line
名城線
Meijo Line
名港線
Meiko Line
鶴舞線
Tsurumai Line
あおなみ線
Aonami Line
勝川駅
Kachigawa Station
瀬戸方面へ
To Seto
⑦岩屋堂公園
Iwayado Park
ナゴヤドーム
Nagoya Dome
③トヨタ博物館
Toyota Automobile Museum
今池
Imaike
東山公園
Higashiyama Koen
リニモ
Linimo
本山
Motoyama
藤が丘
Fujigaoka
モリコロパーク
(ジブリパーク予定地)
Aichi Earth Expo Memorial Park
(Ghibli Park to open in 2022)
⑥東山動植物園
Higashiyama Zoo & Botanical Gardens
名古屋市博物館
Nagoya City Museum
八事
Yagoto

Places to Visit in Nagoya

ラサール領事の 名古屋おすすめスポット

Nagoya Castle
名古屋城
(Nagoya Jo)

P.136 MAP ＝①

Access 5 min walk from "Shiyakusho (City Hall)" station (Meijo Line) Exit 7 ※ About 20 mins by metro from Nagoya Station **Hours** 9:00 to 16:30 (last entry at 16:00) **Closed** December 29 to January 1 **Admission** ￥500

Nagoya Castle is definitely worth a visit. It's one of the largest castles in Japan and the two golden killer whales called "grampus" that decorate its roof have become symbols of the city. After you visit the castle, you can walk through the park that surrounds it and stop in one of the many restaurants you'll find there.

名古屋に来たなら、名古屋城は絶対に訪れるべし。日本のお城でも最大級のもので、天守の屋根にのせられた金のシャチホコは、名古屋のシンボルとなっています。お城を見学したあとは、城をとりまく名城（めいじょう）公園を散策し、園内の飲食店でひと休みするとよいでしょう。

The mascot for Nagoya's football club team is called "Grampus-kun"

Osu District
大須商店街
(Osu Shotengai)

P.136 MAP ＝②

Access Osu Kannon temple is at Exit 2 of Osu Kannon station (Tsurumai Line) ※ About 20 mins by metro from Nagoya station (take the Higashiyama Line from Nagoya, and transfer to the Tsurumai Line at Fushimi station)

Visit Osu and find out for yourself why I call it the "coolest" part of Nagoya. First, stop by the large Osu Kannon Temple to steep yourself in history; then, spend the rest of the day exploring the many interesting shops you'll find in its meandering "Showa style" arcade. Osu also offers a great selection of restaurants so bring your appetite because you'll be tempted!

なぜ私が大須を名古屋でもっとも"クール"な場所というのか―街を一日散策すればわかるはず。大須観音の広い境内で歴史に思いを馳せたあとは、気になるお店が多彩にたちならぶ"昭和"なアーケードをぶらぶら探索してみて。大須には魅力的なレストランもたくさんありますから、おなかをへらして挑みましょう。

Toyota Automobile Museum
トヨタ博物館
(Toyota Hakubutsukan)

P.137 MAP =③

The Nagoya region is one of the most important automotive hubs in the world and this museum represents the city's industrial heritage very well. You'll find not only Toyota cars but many of the most iconic American, French, British and Italian cars dating back more than a century. A must visit for any car buff.

世界でも有数の自動車産業拠点・名古屋の、自動車の発達史を紹介。歴代のトヨタ車だけでなく、世界の名車が多数展示されており、クルマ好きにはたまらない場所です。

Access 5 min walk from "Geidai-dori" station (Linimo) ※ About 40 mins by metro from Nagoya Station (take the Higashiyama Line to the terminus, Fujigaoka station and transfer to Linimo) **Hours** 9:30 to 17:00 (last entry at 16:30) **Closed** Monday (or Tuesday when Monday falls on a public holiday), the Year-end and New Year period **Admission** ¥1,200 for adults, ¥600 for high and middle school students, ¥400 for elementary school students, ¥700 for seniors

LEGOLAND® and the Aquarium
名古屋港エリア
(Nagoya-ko Area)

P.136 MAP =④⑤

Families with young kids will enjoy visiting the port of Nagoya. Beyond boat watching, there'll be plenty to do with both a large aquarium and a fun "building block" themed amusement park located close to each other within the harbor.

小さなお子さんのいるご家庭なら、名古屋港がオススメ。船を眺められるのはもちろん、ガーデンふ頭には名古屋港水族館、金城ふ頭にはレゴ・ブロックのテーマパークがあり、たっぷり遊べます。

LEGOLAND®Japan

Access 5min walk from "Kinjo Futo" station (Aonami Line) ※ About 24 mins by Aonami Line from Nagoya Station ※ For operating days and ticket prices, check the official website

Port of Nagoya Aquarium

Access 5 min walk from "Nagoya-ko" station (Meijo Line) ※ About 25 mins by metro from Nagoya Station (take the Higashiyama Line to Sakae, transfer to the Meijo Line heading for Kanayama and bound for Nagoyako) ※ For operating days, check the official website **Admission** ¥2,030 for adults, ¥1,010 for middle and elementary school students, ¥500 for kids above 4

※金城ふ頭とガーデンふ頭の間は、水上バスで行き来できます。
There's a water bus "Cruise Nagoya" between LEGOLAND and the aquarium.

Higashiyama Zoo & Botanical Gardens
東山動植物園

P.137 MAP ＝⑥

You can spend the day at the Higashiyama Zoo and then drop in its botanical garden to admire the beautiful flowers and plants. There are also a few rides that will entertain young children. End the day by going up the Higashiyama Tower for a sprawling view at the great city of Nagoya!

動物園と、植物園の美しい花や植物が、一日で両方楽しめます。子どもが喜ぶ乗りものも。シメには東山タワーから、足下に広がる名古屋の景色を楽しんで。

Access 3 min walk from "Higashiyama Koen" station Exit 3 (Higashiyama Line) ※ About 20 mins by metro from Nagoya Station **Hours** 9:00 to 16:50 **Closed** Monday **Admission** ￥500

Iwayado Park
岩屋堂公園

P.137 MAP ＝⑦

One of the nicer parks in the city. In the summer, smaller kids will enjoy some water fun in the small river that runs through it. When autumn comes and the leaves change colors, the park becomes an ideal location for a scenic stroll. Enjoy!

名古屋でオススメする公園のひとつです。夏は園内の小川で、子どもたちが水遊び。秋になれば、紅葉狩りの最高のロケーションになります。ぜひ！

Access 20 mins by taxi (will cost about ¥2,000) from "Owari Seto" station (Seto Line) ※ Seto Line departs from Sakae station. Ride is about 40 mins from Sakae to Owari Seto.

Eating Out in Nagoya

ラサール領事の おすすめナゴヤめし

Ankake Spaghetti
あんかけスパゲティ

Nagoya's very own spaghetti. Nagoya replaces tomato sauce with a thick spicy brown sauce and throws in green peppers, onions and bits of sausages... and it works! I mention it in one of the stories in this book. There are a few ankake spaghetti chains in Nagoya such as Yokoi, Karame-tei, and Sole and they're all good. I drop in my neighborhood "Paprika" about once a month. Delicious!

名古屋独特のスパゲティ。トマトソースのかわりに、ピーマン、玉ねぎ、刻んだソーセージの入ったどろっと濃いスパイシーな茶色のソースがかかっているのですが…これがウマい！本の中でも紹介しましたが、名古屋には「ヨコイ」や「からめ亭」、「そ〜れ」といったあんかけスパのチェーン店がいくつかあって、どこもおいしいのです。近所の「パプリカ」には、月に一度は行きますね。むっちゃんこうみゃあよ！

There are many great restaurants in Nagoya offering staples of Japanese cuisine like sushi and ramen. But Nagoya has a few delicacies all its own. Here are a few of my favorite "Nagoya Meshi".

名古屋にはお寿司やラーメンなど、日本の代表的な料理が食べられるおいしいお店がたくさんありますが、ここにしかない名物もいろいろあるのです。私のお気にいり「ナゴヤめし」はこちら…!

Furaibo's tebasaki has a sweet soy flavor

Tebasaki
手羽先

Nagoya is famous for its chicken wings served in a variety of spicy ways. Great finger food when enjoying a few beers with friends. My personal favorite is the dry, crispy type seasoned with salt and pepper. Local chains Furaibo and Yama chan are popular places to enjoy "tebasaki" but many "izakaya" bar-restaurants have them on their menu. Delicious!

名古屋は各店独自に調味された鶏の手羽先で有名です。仲間とわいわいビールを飲むときのおつまみにぴったり。味つけはいろいろで、私はパリッと揚げて塩こしょうしたものが好みです。手羽先のお店として有名なのは、地元チェーンの「風来坊」と「世界の山ちゃん」ですが、他のあちこちの居酒屋のメニューにもあります。むっちゃんこうみゃあよ!

Yama-chan's tebasaki is crispy and spicy

Nagoya Morning
名古屋のモーニング

If you enjoy starting your day in a coffee shop, Nagoya is the city for you! There are coffee shops all around and when you order your morning cup of coffee in Nagoya, you're likely to get toast and a hard-boiled egg at no additional charge. Drop in at Nagoya's very own "Komeda's Coffee" chain for your "Nagoya morning".You might want to spread some sweet bean "ogura" jam on your toast! Delicious!

一日のはじまりは喫茶店から、という方に、名古屋はうってつけ！名古屋は街中に喫茶店がありますが、朝行ってコーヒーをたのむと、トーストにゆで卵が無料でついてくるのです。名古屋発祥の「コメダ珈琲店」で「名古屋モーニング」をぜひお試しあれ。トーストにあんこをのせても、むっちゃんこうみゃあよ！

Miso Katsu
みそカツ

You can enjoy miso in a sauce as well since Nagoya folks like to put "miso" on everything! Pouring thick miso sauce over pork cutlets, called "miso katsu", is one of the most popular ways to enjoy it. There are specialty restaurants offering miso katsu but you'll also find it on the menu of many family restaurants across the city. Delicious!

名古屋人はなんにでも「みそ」をかけるといいますが、そう、みそはソースとしてもおいしい。濃いみそだれをかけたトンカツ「みそカツ」は、その代表選手です。みそカツの専門店もありますが、名古屋中のファミリーレストランで食べることができます。むっちゃんこうみゃあよ ！

Ebi-Furai
えびフライ

Pronounced "ebi friya" while rolling the "r" strongly, these deep-fried battered shrimps have become one of Nagoya's signature foods. You'll find them on the lunch menu of many restaurants in Nagoya. Delicious!

名古屋では「えびフリャー」と呼ばれる、えびのフライも名古屋名物となっており、いろんなお店のランチメニューにあります。むっちゃんこうみゃあよ！

Red Miso Soup
赤だし

Miso soup, made from fermented bean paste, is enjoyed across Japan but there are many regional varieties. In Nagoya, miso soup is generally the dark red type called "aka miso" rather than the lighter type called "shiro miso" generally served in the Tokyo area. The red type has a much richer taste and is enjoyed with practically every meal in Nagoya. Delicious!

豆を発酵させて作る「みそ」からつくった「みそ汁」は、日本中で食べられますが、地域によって特徴があります。東京のほうでは薄い「白みそ」を使うのが一般的ですが、名古屋では濃い色の「赤みそ」を使います。コクのある赤みそは、ほぼ毎食食べられています。むっちゃんこうみゃあよ！

在名古屋領事たちの座談会！

愛知・名古屋の魅力は？

中日新聞朝刊なごや市民版で毎週日曜日に連載している「なごやか外交」。ラサールさんのほか、在名古屋６カ国の外交官に執筆をお願いする、長期連載です。2019 年の年明けに執筆者を集め、「愛知・名古屋を魅力ある街にするには」をテーマに座談会を開きました。

（本記事は 2019 年１月６日、７日に掲載されました）※インタビュー中敬称略

カナダ領事●シェニエ・ラサール

中国総領事●鄧偉（トウ イ）

北京外国語大卒、早稲田大修士号取得。駐大阪副総領事、大使館参事官兼報道官、駐長崎総領事を歴任し、2017 年 10 月から現職。趣味は散策、旅行

韓国総領事●チョン＝ファンソン

日本、英国大使館勤務後、大阪副総領事、札幌総領事などを経て 2016 年 11 月から現職。家族は妻と１男１女。趣味は写真。写真集を出し、個展をひらいたことも。「レンズ越しに東海の美しさや温かさをとりたい 」

ペルー総領事●アントニオ・ミランダ・シスニエガス Antonio Pedro Miranda Sisniegas

2017 年３月から現職。ペルー外交官研修所で外交と国際関係学修士号を、またコスタリカ大通信制で人権修士号を取得。クラシックやジャズが好き。当地では名古屋フィルハーモニー交響楽団の演奏会に出向く

米国首席領事●ゲーリー・シェイファー Gary Schaefer

米国の通信社の記者として東京やバンコクに勤務した後、2005 年に外交官に。2017 年8月から現職。妻子あり。英語、日本語、フランス語が堪能。名古屋人に負けないほどみそカツが大好物。趣味は SL と昭和レトロで、若大将シリーズをほとんど見ていることが自慢

ブラジル副領事●ファビオ・マガリャンイス Fabio L.L. de Magalhães

1976 年リオデジャネイロ市生まれ。サウジアラビアとパラグアイ大使館勤務後、2016 年１月から現職

（聞き手：中日新聞社会部長 吉枝道生）

ー名古屋市が実施した調査で、名古屋は最も魅力がない都市との結果が出ました。名古屋や愛知の魅力をどう感じていますか。

ラサール　どうしてそういう評価がつくのかわかりませんね。私は東京に、妻は京都に住んだことがあり、ふたりともどこに住みたいかというと、名古屋です。特に子育てをして家族とすごすという意味では快適。大都会でなんでもあるが、圧倒されないちょうどよい規模だと思います。大好きなのは大須ですね。若者文化、パソコン、外国人が集まる店など、大須にはすべてあります。

マガリャンイス　ほかの都市に住んだことはないですが、東京、大阪をのぞけば、これだけたくさんのオプションがある街はありません。渋滞もないし、地下鉄でどこにでもいける。公園もたくさんあって、博物館もある。名古屋城や犬山城といった城も魅力的。祭りも、都市部ではサムライの時代にはなかった灰色のビルの前で行われますが、この近辺の祭りはとてもリアルな感じがします。

犬山城　Inuyama Castle

鄧　着任して２年ですが、魅力がないなんていえないですよ。日本の３大都市のひとつで、産業が発達している。日本は島国ですが、名古屋は街も広々と整然としていて、大陸的な街づくりだと感じます。おいしいものもたくさんあります。手羽先にみそ煮込みうどん…。

シェイファー　私が大好きなみそカツも忘れないで！（笑）

鄧　そう、みそカツも（笑）。中国北部の濃い味つけと似ていて、食事はおいしいと思っています。中国との結びつきも強く、中国から中部に訪れる観光客も増えています。

チョン　私が言おうと思ったことは、鄧さんがほとんど話してしまいました（笑）。やはり、ものづくりの街だということ。あとは三英傑もみんな、この地方出身で歴史もある。ただ、韓国人にとって「名古屋」と言われてピンとくるものがないのは課題だと思います。韓国から東京、大阪、札幌、福岡行きのパッケージ旅行はたくさんありますが、名古屋はないのが原因かもしれません。伊勢神宮や白川郷などとパッケージにして売りだすとよいのでは。

名古屋まつりを練り歩く三英傑
3 Feudal lords in Nagoya Matsuri parade

シスニエガス　ペルー人にとっては生活の質がよく、家族の時間がもてる職場がたくさんあるのも魅力的。もっと大都市になると、どちらかが欠けてしまうと思います。名古屋は戦後の再建都市で、どのように都市整備をするかの経験があるのも強みですね。ペルーの外交官が訪れたときは、高速道路などの整備状況におどろいていました。

シェイファー　調査結果はショックでした。簡潔でパッとするコンセプトでＰＲしないといけないと思います。私は、いろんな意味で「セントラル」

と紹介しています。ものづくりの中心。歴史の中心。三英傑もみんな名古屋からでており、名古屋がなければ今の日本はないですよ。食文化も中心だと思う。みそカツなどのあげものを中心に、外国人の口にあうものが多くあります。あるレストランが名古屋メシの英訳メニューを「サムライフード」と訳していたのは、さすがだと思いました。地理的にも中心で、東京、京都にラクに行けるのも強みですね。

大好きなみそカツを手にするシェイファーさん
American Consul with Miso Katsu

ー魅力を伝え、高めるためにどうすればいいと思いますか。

ラサール　名古屋は大阪のように、近隣へのハブ都市になる可能性があると思います。名古屋から京都は決して遠くないし、飛騨高山や白川郷という昔の風景も楽しめる。もちろん名古屋でも、車好きなら、世界中の車が見られるトヨタ博物館が近くにある。熱田神宮、大須などもふくめて、名古屋を中心に１週間ぶんのプランをつくってＰＲしてはどうでしょうか。

鄧　リニア中央新幹線の開通も、ひとつの目玉になりますよね。私は仕事で北陸に行くこともあるが、北陸新幹線ができてとても客が増えている。それと、中国の観光客にとっては、スマホ決済が普及すると便利だと思います。

チョン　名古屋で一番立派だと思った建物は、名駅のモード学園スパイラルタワーズです。非常に近代的で、まさか専門学校とは。名古屋の繊維産業の歴史とあわせて、パリコレのようなファッションショーをやってはどうかと思います。日本一の規模でね。それと、期待しているのはジブリパーク。ジブリは韓国でも人気なので、これが立派なものになれば、韓国人はたくさんきます。

スパイラルタワーズ
Mode Gakuen Spiral Towers

マガリャンイス　日本のドラマを見ると、ほとんど舞台は東京。日本橋、渋谷など、聞いたことがある地名は東京ばかりになってしまいます。名古屋が舞台のドラマや映画がはやれば知名度はあがるはずです。インターネットの時代、日本人にはやるものならすぐにブラジルでもはやる。名古屋に住むブラジル人に手伝ってもらい、観光名所やポルトガル語が通じる店を宣伝するのもよいかも。

シェイファー　市科学館も解説が多言語化されているとよいと思いました。パリのように、複数の観光施設の共通入場券があると便利です。

シスニエガス　名古屋城とトヨタ自動車の最新型車両など、ちがった魅力を組みあわせて売りだすのもいいかもしれません。久屋大通公園を散歩していたら、昔の写真パネルが展示してあって興味深かった。街中に「この場所は 100 年前こうだった」という写真と解説があるとおもしろいと思います。

広小路通と大津通の交差点にある History のパネル
Signboard explaining local history

鄧　中国でトヨタは有名だが、トヨタが愛知にあるとは知らない人も多い。そこをわかりやすく説明してはどうでしょう。

ラサール　トヨタの街、といえば「おお！」となりますよね。コスプレサミットもうまくキープできている。このイベントを奪いたい街はたくさんあるはずです。

コスプレサミット
World Cosplay
Summit in Osu

シェイファー　コスプレサミットも多言語化してほしいです。市民が満足するだけでなく、この街のすばらしさをいかに世界に共有するかも考えてもらいたいですね。

ー新年に行うインタビュー、ということでみなさんの国のお正月のすごし方を教えてください。

ラサール　おおみそかには親戚で集まって、忘年会のような雰囲気で楽しみます。日本でいう紅白歌合戦のような国民的な番組がカナダにもあって、その年の出来事をふりかえりながら、0時前には新年のカウントダウンをします。1月1日は、特に決まったすごし方はなく、31日の夜、つまり「お正月イブ」の方がもりあがりますね。

マガリャンイス　ブラジルもクリスマスにくらべると、パッとしません。日本のようにお年玉もないので。クリスマスは必ず家族ですごし、正月はどこで誰となにをしていても自由。ただ、海岸近くの街ではおおみそかの伝統的な習慣があります。白色の服を身につけて海岸にいき、ヒザまで入水して7つの波を飛びこえると願いがかなうといわれています。アフリカ由来の海の女神イエマンジャに祈る行事でしたが、今はパーティー的な雰囲気ですね。

鄧　中国の正月は旧暦で祝います。中国人にとっては、一家だんらんの一番大切な休息の時間。中国北部では1日午前0時前に水ギョウザを食べます。そのうちひとつかふたつには、アメなどの縁起物が入っています。南部は水ギョウザではなく、めん類です。0時になると、爆竹を鳴らして悪いものを流します。

チョン　韓国も旧暦の正月は前後の1日をあわせて計3日が休みになりますが、西暦の正月は1日だけ。正月の朝には「チャレ」といわれる法事をします。たくさんの食べものをテーブルに用意して、床にしゃがみこんでおじぎして祖先や親にあいさつする「チョル」をすませ、その料理を朝ごはんとして食べます。墓参りをしたあと、日本のすごろくのような遊びですが、「ユッ」というゲームで大人も子どもも一緒になって遊びます。

シスニエガス　国民の80%がキリスト教徒なので、一番大切なのはクリスマスです。12月24日はミサが終わるとおじいちゃんの家に集まって、七面鳥や豚肉、サラダ、「Paneton（パネトン）」というクリスマスケーキをホットチョコレートと一緒に食べるのが習慣ですね。午前2～3時ごろまでクリスマスソングをかけてパーティーを楽しみます。

シェイファー　元日はポテトチップスやお菓子を食べながら「Bowl（ボウル）」とよばれるアメフトの大学選手権決勝をみんなで観戦します。いまでも、あの年はあの大学が勝った負けた、と子どものころの記憶とともに鮮明におぼえていますね。家族でおたがいの新年の決意を聞きあうのも習慣です。

ー日本のお正月はどう感じていますか。

ラサール　印象的なのは正月に見る駅伝ですね。おおみそかの紅白歌合戦は、誰も聞いていない曲のときにチャンネルを変えたら、家族から怒られたことがあります（笑）。カナダでは昔は、正月にお父さんが宗教的な役割を担って「今年１年、健康でいられるように」と家族にBlessing（ブレッシング。祈り、祝福）をしていましたが、いまはなくなりました。日本は初もうでなどの習慣が維持されていて、とてもよいことだと思います。

マガリャンイス　ある年は友人家族と熱田神宮に初もうでに行って、屋台でいろんなものを食べて、神事を見ました。別の年は、０時になって自宅近くの神社に参拝すると、焼きイモとお酒がふるまわれました。その後、大須観音まで歩いたのですが、すごい人の数で、警察官も「待ってください！」などと声をあげて交通整理していて。ああ、これは小さな神社のほうがいいかもなと思いました（笑）。

熱田神宮の初詣には毎年700万人が訪れる
New Year's Day at Atsuta Shrine

シェイファー　日本の正月で好きなのは、こたつに入っておいしいおせち料理を食べること。日本人の義母が３日くらいかけて作ってくれるんです。お年玉もよいですよね。アメリカのクリスマスは物を贈りますが、お年玉は現金。なんでも買える！すばらしい、子どもにとっては超うれしいですよ。

The consuls talk about Nagoya

〈座談会英文まとめ・領事たちのオススメは ？〉

In the previous 8 pages, consuls from 6 countries (Canada, China, Korea, Peru, the USA and Brazil) discussed ways to make Nagoya more appealing. Here are some of the things they highlighted.

Nagoya is a center of Japanese history!

三英傑を輩出した歴史の中心

Festival floats in Higashi ward
名古屋市東区の山車揃え

Nobunaga, Hideyoshi, and Ieyasu, three famous warlords who played leading roles in Japan's Sengoku period (1467-1615 " Warring States Period") were all born in Nagoya. They are still remembered in many movies and television series and you can even see them walking the streets of Nagoya during the Nagoya Matsuri held in October. There are many traditional festivals in Nagoya and Aichi that are rooted in traditions passed on for centuries.

Atsuta Shrine where one of the Three Sacred Treasures of Japan, the "Kusanagi-no-Tsurugi" sword, is kept has been revered since ancient times.

Nagoya is a center of industry!

整備された、ものづくりの中心

Besides being the hometown of Toyota, Nagoya is also known for other industries such as textiles, ceramics, steel and machinery. The consuls praised Nagoya's wide roads and easy to navigate grid.

Despite being a big city, Nagoya remains manageable, even comfortable, with less traffic, convenient subway service, many parks and facilities; a great place for families.

Nagoya, as a hub to other cities!
近隣へのハブ都市

Historical sites you can easily access from Nagoya

Inuyama Castle 犬山城

Built in 1537 atop a hill that overlooks the Kiso River, Inuyama Castle has the oldest "tenshu" (tower) in Japan where you can enjoy the beautiful scenery.

Access 30 mins by train from Nagoya

Hikone Castle 彦根城

Its tenshu is a national treasure just like Inuyama Castle.

Access 90 mins by train from Nagoya

Hikone Castle 彦根城

Ise Shrine 伊勢神宮

Every year, 8 million pilgrims visit this shrine dedicated to the sun goddess, Amaterasu. You will enjoy the beautiful sacred woods around the shrine.

Access 90 mins by train from Nagoya

Must visit sites accessible from Nagoya

Shirakawa go 白川郷

A mountain village registered as a UNESCO heritage site. This snowy village is famous for the thatched rooves of its traditional gassho style houses.

Access 180 mins by highway bus from Nagoya

Rice planting in Shirakawa go
白川郷の田植えの様子

Takayama 飛騨高山

A beautiful old town that has preserved much of its Edo period charm. The city is very popular with foreign visitors who also enjoy its hot springs and pristine nature.

Access 150 mins by train or highway bus from Nagoya

「領事の故郷・モントリオールの魅力を紹介！」

モントリオールは島！

モントリオールはセント・ローレンス川の真ん中に浮かぶ大きな川中島。つまり、周縁に沿って延々と美しい川の景色が楽しめるわけです。ただ、島がゆえの欠点もあります。島の外に位置する郊外からモントリオールへ通勤する人が多いため、朝と夜のラッシュ時は、島に向かう橋が大混雑となってしまいます…。

島の真ん中には山！

モントリオールという地名は、島の真ん中にある小さな緑深い山「モン・ロワイヤル（フランス語で“王の山”）」に由来します。つまりこの緑の楽園が眺められるポイントが、街中にあるわけです。山は公園になっていて、山頂からきれいな街の景色を眺めることもできます。

ごはんがおいしい！

モントリオールに多いのは、フランス系カナダ人。すなわち、多くのレストランでおいしいワインとチーズが愉しめます。

そもそもカナダには地球上のあらゆる人種が集まっているので、モントリオールには中華料理、ギリシャ料理、レバノン料理、イタリア料理…と、世界中の食べ物がそろっています。私の個人的なお気にいりは、スモークミートのサンドイッチ。西欧からのユダヤ移民が持ちこんだ、モントリオールの名物料理です。有名店はシュワルツやレスターズ、ニッケルズ。「ミディアム・ファット」のサンドイッチに、ディル漬けのピクルスとポテトフライをつけあわせで注文してみて…オススメを聞いておいてよかった！と思うはず。うみゃあですよ。

ナイトライフが充実！

フランス系カナダ人は、ノリがラテン系。外食と夜遊びが大好きです。世界のビールにウィスキー、ワインを飲み明かし、踊り明かしたいなら、ぜひモントリオールへ！いろんなジャンルのクラブやカフェがそろっていますよ。

Great things about my hometown of Montreal

It's an island!

Montreal is a large island in the middle of the Saint Lawrence River. That means that you can enjoy beautiful river scenery all along its long coastline.

There is a drawback though, many people commute to Montreal from its many suburbs located off the island of Montreal, so its many bridges are very congested in the morning and evening rush hours…

There's a mountain in the middle of that island!

That's right, Montreal actually gets its name from "le Mont Royal" (French for "Mount Royal") the small green mountain that rises in the middle of the island. That means that in many parts of the city, you can enjoy a view of this green oasis. Better yet, you can visit Mount Royal Park at the top of the mountain and enjoy a fantastic view of the city.

The food is great

French Canadians are the biggest ethnic group in Montreal so you'll find that the wine and cheese selection in many restaurants is very good. But Canadians come from almost every corner of the planet, and what's even better is that they brought their food with them to Montreal!

Chinese food, Greek food, Lebanese food, Italian food, you'll find it all in Montreal! My personal favorite is the "smoked meat sandwich" (immigrants from Jewish communities in Eastern Europe brought this delicacy to my city). Go to Schwartz's, Lester's or Nickels and ask for a "medium fat" smoked meat sandwich with a dill pickle and fries. You'll thank me later. It's delicious!

The nightlife is great

French Canadians are a latin people, so we love to eat out and also go out. If you enjoy spending the evening dancing with friends or enjoying beers, whiskeys and wines from every corner of the world, you've come to the right place! There are nightclubs and cafes to suit every taste.

Thank you

Rika Tanaka who was my first collaborator and believed in the crazy project of me becoming a columnist for the Chunichi newspaper!

Chikako Onabe and Asako Saito who helped me with many of the translations.

Nagasaka san from the Chunichi who gave me good advice when I started to write my column.

Mai Sato who thought my story would make an interesting book – and led this project.

My kids, Sakura, Taro and Momoko for being an endless source of "stories" (neta).

My wife Noriko who was the true "editor in chief" of my columns. In many ways, she is the "voice" you hear when you read my stories in Japanese.

Thank you all!

...and thank you Nagoya for being a great place to raise a family!

おわりに

あとがきにかえて、お世話になったみなさんに感謝の気持ちをお伝えします。

在名古屋カナダ領事館ではじめてともに働き、中日新聞の連載を書くなんてクレイジーな企画を後押ししてくれた田中里佳さん。

翻訳を手伝ってくれた、同領事館の大鍋千香子さん、斉藤麻子さん。

連載を書き始めたころ、アドバイスをくれた中日新聞社会部の長坂さん。

連載をまとめたら面白い本になると考え、出版企画を進めた中日新聞出版部の佐藤さん。

たえまなくネタを提供してくれる子どもたち、さくら、太朗、ももこ。

そして私の記事の、真の「編集長」である妻・紀子。私の文章は彼女の「声」でもあります。

みなさん、ありがとう!!

それから名古屋に、家族を育んでくれたこのすばらしい土地に、ありがとう!!

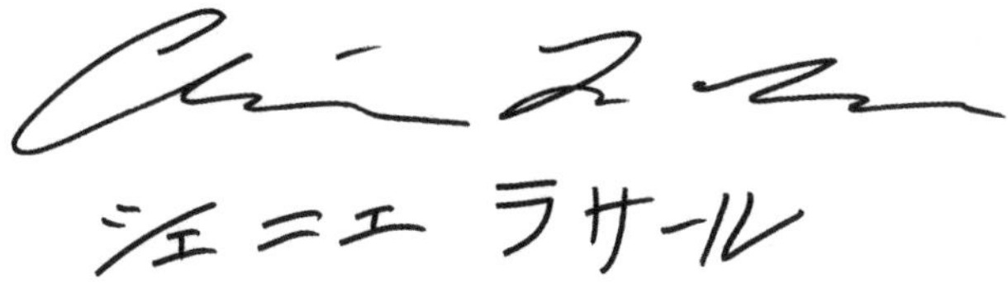

在名古屋カナダ領事館
領事 兼 通商代表

シェニエ・ラサール
Chénier La Salle

ケベック州、モントリオール出身。
1990年オタワ大学で法律の学位を取得。92年弁護士資格を取得。弁護士として就職した後、再びモントリオール大学に入り、東アジア研究の学位を取得。94～95年、留学生として南山大学で日本語を習得。その後、名古屋大学法学部へと進み、日本の政治経済を学ぶ。2000年に同大学大学院法学修士号を取得した後、04年まで日本企業にて勤務。
日本メープルリーフフーズ株式会社での民間企業業務を経験し、アルバータ州政府の対日貿易ディレクターを務める。カナダビーフ輸出連合会の副会長を務めた後、外務省に入省。
家族は妻と3人の子供。趣味は創作することで、日本で英会話本を2冊出版。ボードゲーム作成で、アメリカとヨーロッパでGame of the Year受賞。

ラサール領事のなごや日記

2020年2月10日　初版第1刷発行

著　者	シェニエ・ラサール
ブックデザイン	株式会社エディマート
イラスト	株式会社インディーグラフィック
発行者	勝見 啓吾
発行所	中日新聞社
	住所 〒460-8511 名古屋市中区三の丸一丁目6番1号
	TEL.052-201-8811（大代表）
	TEL.052-221-1714（出版部直通）
	郵便振替　00890-0-10番
	ホームページ　http://www.chunichi.co.jp/nbook/
印　刷	図書印刷株式会社

定価はカバーに表示してあります。乱丁・落丁本はお取り替えいたします。

ISBN 978-4-8062-0762-7　C0082